MURDER MYSTERY, GRAPHIC NOVELS, AND MORE

MURDER MYSTERY, GRAPHIC NOVELS,
AND MORE

Innovative Programs for Engaging Teens in Your Library

Thane Benson

 LIBRARIES
UNLIMITED™

An Imprint of ABC-CLIO, LLC
Santa Barbara, California • Denver, Colorado

Library of Congress Control Number: 2019021178

ISBN: 978-1-4408-6136-9 (paperback)
　　　 978-1-4408-6137-6 (ebook)

23　22　21　20　19　　1　2　3　4　5

This book is also available as an eBook.

Libraries Unlimited
An Imprint of ABC-CLIO, LLC

ABC-CLIO, LLC
147 Castilian Drive
Santa Barbara, California 93117
www.abc-clio.com

This book is printed on acid-free paper ∞

Manufactured in the United States of America

This book is dedicated to the staff of the Denver Public Library.
You inspire me every day with your creativity and passion.
Thanks for making work fun.

CONTENTS

HI, MY NAME IS THANE. I'M A LIBRARIAN.

LIKE MOST LIBRARIANS, MY JOB REQUIRES ME TO PROVIDE A BROAD RANGE OF SERVICES TO PEOPLE OF ALL AGES.

I DO READER'S ADVISORY, ANSWER REFERENCE QUESTIONS, PERFORM STORYTIMES, AND TEACH TECHNOLOGY, AMONG OTHER THINGS.

BUT WHAT I ENJOY THE MOST ABOUT MY JOB IS WORKING WITH TEENS. AND IN PARTICULAR, WHAT I'M PASSIONATE ABOUT IS ENGAGING TEENS' CREATIVITY.

I DO THIS THROUGH CREATIVE PROGRAMMING THAT ENABLES TEENS TO EXPRESS THEMSELVES HOWEVER THEY--

HEY!

WHAT'S GOING ON HERE?

I'M DOING THE INTRODUCTION TO THE BOOK.

INTRODUCTION? WHAT DO YOU MEAN INTRODUCTION? INTRODUCTIONS TO BOOKS ARE JUST PAGES OF TEXT THAT NOBODY READS. THEY DON'T HAVE WEIRD LITTLE DRAWINGS AND WORD BALLOONS AND BOXES. THIS LOOKS MORE LIKE A... A... A COMIC BOOK!

EXACTLY. I'M TRYING TO PRESENT INFORMATION IN A MORE DYNAMIC, ACCESSIBLE MANNER.

I THOUGHT THIS WAS AN INSTRUCTIONAL TEXT! IS THIS WHOLE FREAK'N TOME JUST A BIG COMIC BOOK?!!

NO. JUST PORTIONS OF THE BOOK ARE PRESENTED LIKE THIS.

IF YOU JUST SKIP AHEAD A FEW PAGES YOU CAN SEE: MOST OF THIS BOOK IS JUST WORDS.

OH, THANK GOODNESS. THAT MAKES ME FEEL SO MUCH BETTER. I DON'T KNOW ABOUT THIS WHOLE COMIC BOOK THING...

y can start
ng intelligible.
t saying anything
ch actor plays the
s into English. If you
nes of all the actors.

ON THE CONTRARY, ANIMATION IS ALL ABOUT CREATING THE ILLUSION OF MOVEMENT WITH STILL IMAGES. BY FLIPPING THROUGH THE PAGES QUICKLY, WE CAN CREATE THE ILLUSION OF MOVEMENT. THERE ARE LOTS OF WAYS TO CREATE DIFFERENT ANIMATIONS. A FLIP BOOK IS JUST ONE EXAMPLE. WE'LL EXPLORE THIS, IN DEPTH, IN CHAPTER FOUR: ANIMATION.

OOOOH...

SO LIKE I WAS SAYING, I'M PASSIONATE ABOUT DOING CREATIVE PROGRAMMING WITH TEENS. THE POINT OF THIS BOOK IS TO TO MAP OUT HOW IT'S ALL DONE, SO YOU, THE READER, CAN DO THE SAME. IN CHAPTER ONE OF THE THIS BOOK WE'LL EXPLORE DIFFERENT CREATIVITY GAMES TO KICK-START TEENS' IMAGINATIONS. THESE GAMES RUN THE GAMUT FROM MINUTE-LONG ICEBREAKERS TO GAMES THAT COULD, IN THEORY, TAKE HOURS TO COMPLETE.

IN CHAPTER TWO WE'LL TALK ABOUT GRAPHIC NOVEL PRODUCTION. IN CHAPTER THREE WE'LL DISCUSS HOW TO CREATE MURDER MYSTERY EVENTS THAT --

MURDER?!! YOU'RE GOING TO TEACH TEENAGERS HOW TO MURDER?!!

WHAT KIND OF A BOOK IS THIS?!!

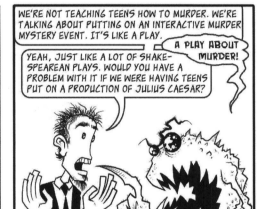

WE'RE NOT TEACHING TEENS HOW TO MURDER. WE'RE TALKING ABOUT PUTTING ON AN INTERACTIVE MURDER MYSTERY EVENT. IT'S LIKE A PLAY.

A PLAY ABOUT MURDER!

YEAH, JUST LIKE A LOT OF SHAKE-SPEAREAN PLAYS. WOULD YOU HAVE A PROBLEM WITH IT IF WE WERE HAVING TEENS PUT ON A PRODUCTION OF JULIUS CAESAR?

DON'T YOU BRING THE BARD INTO THIS! I OUGHTA' MURDER YOU!

HEY! WAIT! WHAT ARE YOU--?!!

NOT SO MUCH FUN NOW, IS IT?

AAAHHHH!

CHAPTER ONE

CREATIVITY GAMES
HAVING FUN WITH WORDS AND PICTURES

THE DICTIONARY DEFINES CREATIVITY AS "THE USE OF THE IMAGINATION OR ORIGINAL IDEAS, ESPECIALLY IN THE PRODUCTION OF AN ARTISTIC WORK." AS CHILDREN, WE'RE EFFORTLESSLY CREATIVE. PLAY IS A CREATIVE ACT. ALL CHILDREN ARE INSTINCTIVELY CREATIVE BECAUSE ALL CHILDREN PLAY INSTINCTIVELY. AS WE GROW OLDER, WE TEND TO PLAY LESS, AND AS A RESULT, WE HAVE LESS OPPORTUNITY TO BE CREATIVE. WHAT YOU WILL FIND IN THIS SECTION ARE GAMES THAT YOU CAN PLAY AS A GROUP, WHICH WILL SPARK CREATIVITY AND GET YOUR IMAGINATION GOING.

IF WE WANTED TO, WE COULD FILL A WHOLE BOOK WITH CREATIVITY GAMES. THERE ARE A LOT OF GREAT GAMES OUT THERE. BUT WE'RE GOING TO LIMIT THIS SECTION TO 20 GAMES. THESE 20 GAMES ARE THE BEST OF THE BEST. THEY ARE THE MOST FUN, ENGAGING, AND SUCCESSFUL CREATIVITY GAMES I HAVE PLAYED WITH GROUPS OF TEENS. THESE GAMES INCLUDE ICEBREAKERS, CREATIVE WRITING PROMPTS, PARTY GAMES, AND IMPROV EXERCISES. ALL OF THESE GAMES MADE THEIR WAY TO ME BY WORD OF MOUTH. I DID NOT INVENT ANY OF THESE GAMES. BUT SOME OF THEM I HAVE MODIFIED AFTER PLAYING TO IMPROVE THE OVERALL EXPERIENCE OF THE GAME. MANY OF THESE GAMES HAVE MANY VARIATIONS. I'VE TRIED TO DESCRIBE THE BEST VERSIONS OF THESE GAMES THAT I'VE HAD THE PLEASURE OF PLAYING.

THE GAMES IN THIS SECTION HAVE BEEN BROKEN DOWN INTO THREE CATEGORIES BASED ON THE ESTIMATED TIME THEY TAKE TO PLAY: **QUICK GAMES** (5–10 MINUTES LONG), **MEDIUM GAMES** (15–20 MINUTES LONG) & **LONG GAMES** (30 MINUTES OR LONGER). THE QUICK GAMES CAN BE USED AS ICE-BREAKERS. THE MEDIUM GAMES CAN BE PARTS OF PROGRAMS. THE LONG GAMES COULD BE ENTIRE PROGRAMS IN THEM-SELVES. ALL THE GAMES OUTLINED HERE WILL ENGAGE YOUR IMAGINATION.

MOST OF THE GAMES DESCRIBED HERE REQUIRE NO SUPPLIES WHAT-SOEVER. SOME OF THESE GAMES REQUIRE PENCILS AND PAPER. A FEW OF THESE GAMES REQUIRE COMMON PROPS YOU CAN EASILY FIND—

UNLESS YOU'RE STRANDED ON A DESERT ISLAND, WHICH WOULD BE VERY UNFORTUNATE, ESPECIALLY IF THIS IS THE ONLY BOOK YOU HAVE. BUT ON THE PLUS SIDE, THIS BOOK DOES HAVE A FLIP BOOK, SO, YOU KNOW, THAT SHOULD KEEP YOU ENTERTAINED FOR A GOOD 30 SECONDS OR SO WHILE YOU WAIT FOR THE RESCUE SHIPS TO FINALLY ARRIVE.

CREATIVE PEOPLE TEND TO BE PLAYFUL BY NATURE. SOME PEOPLE LIKEN CREATIVITY TO A MUSCLE. THESE GAMES ARE EXERCISE FOR THAT MUSCLE. IT'S EASY. IT'S FUN. SO COME ON, LET'S FLEX OUR MUSCLES AND START GETTING CREATIVE WITH GAMES!

QUICK GAMES (5–10 MINUTES)

1. ABC STORYTELLING

Estimated time to play: 5 minutes
Supplies needed: None (or Scrabble tiles for the Scrabble variation)
Ideal number of players: At least 4

How It Works

Everyone knows the game where you tell a story as a group, each person telling one sentence of the story. This is that same game but with a great twist.

To begin, have everyone sit in a circle, and select a player to start. You're going to tell a story as a group, each person saying only one sentence of the story, but each sentence will start with a word that starts with a consecutive letter of the alphabet. The first person will start with the letter A. Keep going until you reach Z. If you have less than 26 people playing, keep going around the circle until you reach Z. The real challenge of this game is for whoever gets Z at the end to wrap up the story in one sentence (starting with a word that starts with Z).

For example, a story might sound something like this:

> **A** long time ago, there lived a witch in a cave.
> **B**eneath the cave, underground, there slept a dragon.
> **C**arefully, the witch went about her business, trying to be as quiet as she could be so as to not wake the dragon.
> **D**uring a thunderstorm, the dragon awoke!
> . . .

And so on and so forth until someone has to end the story with something like this:

> **Z**ebras across the world neighed with joy when they heard the dragon had been slain.

A variation of this same game can be played with Scrabble tiles. Pass the bag of Scrabble tiles around the circle and have each player select, without looking, one letter tile from the bag. That player must begin their sentence of the story with a word that begins with the letter on the Scrabble tile.

2. FINDING COMMON GROUND

Estimated time to play: 5 minutes
Supplies needed: None
Ideal number of players: At least 5

How It Works

This is an improv game that's fun and often produces very funny results. As with all improv games, the key to playing the game is to just respond without thinking too much. Have everyone sit in a circle. Ask the group to start shouting out nouns—any nouns. Pick any two nouns you hear. For the best results, pick two nouns that are very different from each other. As an example, we're going to say that you picked telephone and soup.

Explain that this is a word-association game. The goal of the game is for players to come up with a noun that is halfway between the other two nouns. So for our example, they need to come up with something that's halfway between a telephone and soup. "What do you mean halfway between a telephone and soup?" I can hear you asking right now. "There's nothing that's halfway between telephone and soup." You're right. There is nothing obvious that's halfway between a telephone and soup. You have to use your imagination. That's the whole point of the game.

If we were going to pick a super easy example, we might say, what's halfway between the grass and the sky? You might say "a tree" or "a bird." Does that make sense? Another way to think about it is, what do these two words have in common? Okay, it gets a little harder with more disparate nouns.

So to get back to our first example, we're starting with "a telephone" and "soup." The first two players in the circle face each other and, on the count of three, have to yell at the same time what they each think is halfway between a telephone and soup. In this example, we're going to say Player 1 yells "mouth" and at the same time Player 2 yells "house." Okay, great. Now we have two new nouns. Now Player 3 and Player 4 face each other. On the count of three, they both yell out what they think is halfway between "mouth" and "house." Player 3 yells "refrigerator!" and Player 4 yells "toothbrush!" Then we move on to Player 5 and Player 6. On the count of three, they each have to yell out what they think is halfway between "refrigerator" and "toothbrush." And so on . . .

In theory, as you play the game, you will get closer and closer with your nouns, so eventually two players will shout out the same word at the same time. When that happens, it'll be incredibly exciting. Trust me. For our example, we're going to say when Player 7 and Player 8 both yell out what they think is halfway between "refrigerator" and "toothbrush," on the count of three, they are both going to yell "water!" Yay! We won!

The trick to this game is to not overthink it and just shout something, anything, on the count of three. Players might shout crazy things that will make it even harder to come up with something that is halfway between both nouns. That's okay. Just keep going with it. You'll get there eventually. I promise.

3. ONCE UPON A TIME, THERE WAS A BAG

Estimated time to play: 5 minutes
Supplies needed: An assortment of random objects and a bag to hold them in
Ideal number of players: At least 4

How It Works

This is another variation on a communal storytelling game. Each person tells one sentence of a story. But in this version, players must relate their one-sentence contributions to objects they pull from a bag.

First you need a bag. Then you need to fill the bag with random items. Whatever you have lying around will work as long as you have decently diverse items. You could put a shoe in the bag, a pencil, a banana, a desk fan, a pair of sunglasses, a weird mug—you get the idea. Anything will work, but the stranger the object, the better. I would suggest putting about 20 items in the bag or, if you have a large group of players, at least enough items that each player gets two turns.

Sit in a circle, and select a player to go first. The first player starts the story by saying "Once upon a time . . ." and then reaches into the bag, without looking at the contents, and pulls one object out at random. That player must finish the sentence by incorporating whatever object they pull out of the bag into the story somehow. The bag then gets passed to the right, and the next player reaches into the bag, without looking, and pulls out another object. They must continue the story with a sentence that relates to their selected item. The play continues to the right until the last object is removed from the bag and then that player must conclude the story using that object somehow.

For example, Player 1 pulls out a mug with the image of a kitten on it and says, "Once upon a time, there was an old woman who had a large collection of novelty mugs."

Player 2 pulls a toy dinosaur from the bag and says, "This old lady had a pet dinosaur that she liked to take for walks in the afternoon."

Player 3 pulls a pair of scissors of the bag and says, "While the old woman and her dinosaur were out walking one day, it started raining scissors from the sky for no reason whatsoever."

And so on until there are no more objects left in the bag. Players are not allowed to look into the bag and pick their items. The challenge and the fun of this game is incorporating unexpected items into the story. Players can reach into the bag and feel around and select an item by touch. But whatever comes out of the bag, that player is stuck with it; they cannot return the item and choose again. Players are free to interpret their items as creatively as they can. In our example, player 2 does not literally say there is a toy dinosaur in the story. Instead, they brought a living, breathing dinosaur into the narrative. Creativity is the whole point and should be encouraged.

4. LAST WORD/FIRST WORD

Estimated time to play: 5 minutes
Supplies needed: None
Ideal number of players: At least 5

How It Works

This is another communal storytelling game. But this game is free of the need to adhere to any narrative constraints. Have your players sit in a circle. Explain that you are going to go around the circle and each say one sentence. The sentence can be anything. It doesn't have to relate to anything. It doesn't even need to make sense. The only rule is your sentence has to start with the last word of the sentence the player before you said. Don't overthink it; just say whatever sentence pops up in your head.

For example:

Player 1: I like macaroni and cheese.
Player 2: Cheese does not grow on trees.

Player 3: Trees provide shade.
Player 4: Shade is my favorite color.

And so on. This is more of a spoken word or poetry exercise than a fiction-writing activity. It can take a few rounds to get players comfortable. The goal is to get to the point where your players just spit out lines without even thinking.

This is a good opener to use as an icebreaker to get a group interacting with a simple word-association game before moving on to something else. This game requires listening to others, which is always a good exercise.

5. LEAST FAVORITE ACROSTIC POEMS

Estimated time to play: 10 minutes
Supplies needed: Pens and paper
Ideal number of players: 1–99

How It Works
Acrostic poems are a staple of grade school–level poetry. An acrostic poem is a type of poetry where one letter in each line (usually the first letter) can be read from top to bottom to spell out a particular word or phrase. Here is a lousy example:

Poets are
Ornery
Every
Month, when the rent comes due

I don't think it's possible to make it out of elementary school without writing at least one acrostic poem about yourself that spells out your first name. An acrostic poem is a somewhat overused and tired creative exercise that can be perceived as juvenile. But this game breathes new life into an old classic.

Start the game by asking players to write down their least favorite word. You need a word that they find phonetically displeasing. If they have a hard time coming up with something, have them brainstorm things they don't like, until they come up with a word that they don't even like to say. Ideally it is the sound of the word more than its meaning that is distasteful, but it can be both.

Once your players have selected a word, have them write it down vertically, writing one letter per line. And then have them write an acrostic poem describing the word or why they don't like the word. Strictly speaking, the letters of their selected least favorite word don't have to be the first letter of each line. They just have to appear somewhere in the line. Generally speaking, the fewer words per line, the better the acrostic poem. The poem can tell a narrative (like the previous "Poem" example) or just a collection of related words (see the following example).

"Moist" is often cited as the least favorite word in the English language whenever there is a poll on that sort of thing. So let's use it as an example. Here is an acrostic poem describing the word "moist."

Mucus
Oily
Insidious
Sticky
Touch

If you are some sort of an insufferable optimist, you can flip this game on its head and have players write down their favorite words instead and make acrostic poems out of them. But it's way more fun to use your least favorite word, and I guarantee you'll get better poetry going negative. Artists have to suffer for their art, after all.

6. STORY FILLER

Estimated time to play: 10 minutes
Supplies needed: Pens and two slips of paper per person
Ideal number of players: At least 5

How It Works

Give all your players two slips of paper. On one slip of paper, have them write the opening line to a story. On the other slip, have them write the last sentence of a story. Put the beginnings in a hat and the endings in other hats. Randomly draw one slip of paper from each. Read the beginning and the ending of the story. Have your players line up in a line. Give the beginning slip to the first player in line and the ending slip to the last player. The goal of this game is to get from the beginning to the ending in some logical manner, with each player adding one sentence. Have the first player read the opening line of the story again and then have them add one more sentence to the story. Continue down the line, with each player adding one sentence to the story until you reach the last player. That player adds one last sentence and then reads the ending.

It's okay if it doesn't work out the first time. Draw another beginning and ending from the hat and try again. This is a great creativity challenge that really requires teamwork and listening to solve a creative problem as a team.

7. THE EXQUISITE CORPSE

Estimated time to play: 10 minutes
Supplies needed: Pens and paper
Ideal number of players: 3 or more

How It Works

Exquisite Corpse is parlor game, invented by surrealist artists in the 1920s. There are many versions of this game that all bear the name Exquisite Corpse. The original Exquisite Corpse was a writing game where each player added a sentence to a written story. As the story goes, the first game began when a French Surrealist wrote "The exquisite corpse shall drink the new wine" and then passed the piece of paper to his Parisian buddy to continue the story.

The game can also be played as a drawing exercise. It can be played as a body drawing game or as a completely free-form drawing game or as some sort of combination of both games.

To play the body drawing game, fold a piece of paper in thirds. Have Player 1 draw some feet and legs in the bottom third of the piece of paper. It doesn't have to be human legs. In fact, they could be the legs of a completely imaginary creature. Player 1's drawing should just barely cross over the folded line (just a millimeter or two). Then fold the paper so the drawing cannot be seen, other than the one or two millimeters that cross over the fold. Player 2 takes the paper and continues the drawing, using the millimeter or two of visible drawing as a starting point to begin drawing the torso of the body. Again, Player 2 should just barely draw a millimeter or two beyond the next fold. Then, again, the paper should be folded, such that just the last third is visible, and then passed on to Player 3, who will continue the drawing to complete the head. Once Player 3 is finished, the paper is unfolded, and the body of the exquisite corpse is revealed (see example in Figure 1.1).

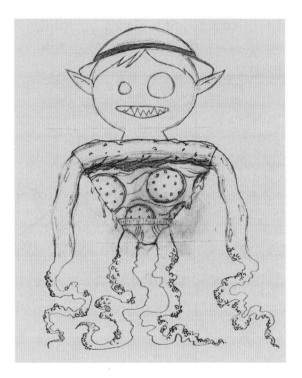

Figure 1.1

To play the free-form version of exquisite corpse, fold a piece of paper three or four times and have Player 1 start drawing whatever they would like, again going just millimeter or two over the fold line with their drawing. Fold the paper to hide the drawing and pass it on to the next player. The game proceeds exactly like the body version, but at the end of the game you are going to reveal something much stranger and much more surreal than the body of an exquisite corpse (see example in Figure 1.2).

Instead of having your group of players sitting around waiting for the folded paper to be passed to them while only one person draws, you can play the Multiple Corpse variation of this game. Have your players sit at a table in a circle, each with their own paper and pen. Have each player start their own Exquisite Corpse drawing, limit the drawing time to a couple of minutes, and then have everyone pass at once. In this version you don't ever have to wait to draw, and at the end of the game, you will have multiple Exquisite Corpses.

Figure 1.2

8. THE INFAMOUS CHAINSAW TELEPHONE MASSACRE SILENT MOVIE

Estimated time to play: 10 minutes
Supplies needed: None
Ideal number of players: 5 or more

How It Works

This is an improv game that's a fresh take on the old playground game, Telephone. In Telephone, players sit in a circle, whisper a phrase into each other's ears, and repeat the phrase, from one player to each other until it reaches the final player in the circle. At the end of Telephone, the payoff is to hear the last person recite the phrase out loud, and all laugh at how much it changed over the course of the game. The Infamous Chainsaw Telephone Massacre Silent Movie is just like that but with added charades and a murder mystery mixed in to spice things up a bit.

This is not a game for the easily embarrassed. This game requires looking like a complete fool in front of other players. I would not recommend playing this game with a group that just met—unless, of course, this group of strangers happens to be extremely dramatic and comfortable in their skins. This is not an icebreaker game. This is a game best played with a group of people who know each other and are comfortable with one another. If you have the right group, this game can be hysterically fun. With the wrong group, it can be a very awkward experience. You won't really know which one it'll be until you try. So give it a try!

Explain to all the players that there has been a murder. Someone, somewhere, has committed the act of murder using a murder weapon. All players must solve the murder without speaking, through pantomime. Player 1 decides three things:

1. What the murderers' profession is (i.e., butler, plumber, lawyer, librarian, etc.)
2. Where the murder took place (i.e., ballroom, bowling alley, firehouse, movie theater, etc.)
3. What the murder weapon was (i.e., knife, poison, piano, guillotine, etc.).

Player 1 should write all three things down but should not reveal them to any other player. All other players leave the room. The players then enter the room one at a time. Player 1 must pantomime the three clues to Player 2. Neither player should speak. Beginning with the murderer's profession, Player 1 has 30 seconds to communicate this information through gestures without speaking or making noises, just like in charades. If Player 2 thinks they understand the murderer's profession, they can nod and then Player 1 can move on to the second piece of information: where the murder took place. After 30 seconds, Player 1 must move on to where the murder took place whether or not Player 2 understands the murderer's profession. Again, Player 1 has 30 seconds to communicate the location of the murder through pantomime. Player 2 can nod when they think they understand the location so as to move the game forward or after 30 seconds. Player 1 must move on to the third piece of information: the murder weapon. This is the final piece of information that must be communicated silently through gestures. When Player 2 thinks they understand or when 30 seconds has passed (whichever comes first), Player 2 will "take" the murder weapon from Player 1 and pantomime murdering that player with it. The murdered player has a seat, and Player 3 comes into the room.

Now it's Player 2's turn to pantomime all three pieces of the murder mystery for Player 3. At the end, Player 3 "takes" the murder weapon and pantomimes murdering Player 2. In comes Player 4, and the game continues in this fashion until you reach the last player. At the end of the game, the last player announces what they believe the murderer's profession to be, where the murder took place, and what the murder weapon was. Player 1 then reveals the original three pieces of information. Then all players have a good laugh at how convoluted the story of the murder mystery became through all the pantomime retellings. If you wish, you can perform a "postmortem" and go backward from player to player and have each player explain what they were trying to communicate until you reach the beginning. Personal interpretation or misinterpretation, as it may be, is at the heart of what makes this game so fun. The goal of the game is not to faithfully interpret and reproduce each player's pantomime. Rather, this game is meant to be a celebration of the inherent creativity we all possess in taking in information and then expressing that information in our own unique fashion.

MEDIUM GAMES (15–20 MINUTES)

9. THE AUTHOR AND THE EDITOR

Estimated time to play: 15 minutes
Supplies needed: None
Ideal number of players: 2 or more

How It Works

This is a storytelling game that is a variation of a classic improv game sometimes called "Take it Back."

Have your participants pair off in twos. The players will each take turns being the Author and the Editor. It is the Author's job to tell a story. It is the Editor's job to change the story (not necessarily for the better). The game begins with the Author starting their story. Whenever the Editor feels like it, they shout, "Change it!" The Author then repeats the last sentence they said, changing the last word or phrase. The Editor may repeat "Change it!" as many times as they like, forcing the Author to keep changing the last word of phrase of their story. The only words the Editor may say while the story is being told is "Change it!" The Editor is not allowed to give any sort of suggestion. If the Editor says nothing, the Author continues the story. The Author must keep telling the story until the Editor says, "I love it!" signaling the end of the story.

For example:

Author: "This is a story about a mouse."
Editor: "Change it!"
Author: "This is a story about a cat."
Editor: "Change it!"
Author: "This is a story about a dolphin."
Editor: ". . ."
Author: "This dolphin's name was Frank."
Editor: ". . ."
Author: "Frank lived in the ocean."
Editor: "Change it!"
Author: "Frank lived in an aquarium."
Editor: "Change it!"
Author: "Frank lived in a swimming pool."
Editor: ". . ."
Author: "Frank dreamed that one day he would be an astronaut."
Editor: "Change it!"
Author: "Frank dreamed that one day he would be a ballerina."
Editor: "Change it!"
Author: "Frank dreamed that one day he would be a professional football player."
Editor: "Change it!"
Author: "Frank dreamed that one day he would be a plastic surgeon."

And so on, until the story comes to its natural conclusion and the Editor shouts out, "I love it!" You can also impose a time limit of two to three minutes if players are going on too long. Then have the players switch and assume opposite roles.

Instruct your Editors that they can't constantly shout "Change it!" They have to let the Authors get a few sentences in a row now and then, without being interrupted. If the Authors are stuck on how to start their story, advise them that they can always start with an autobiographical story. "Yesterday, I . . ." can work as a story prompt. When everyone has finished, have each player retell their edited story to the group.

This is a great creative exercise because it requires a lot of on-the-spot improvisation but with low stakes. The challenge of changing your narrative in flash form where you think the story might be going is a great exercise in flexibility and teaches players to live in the moment, which, of course, is the single most important aspect of all improv acting.

This game can also be played as a more traditional improv performance. It works best with small groups of two or three Actors (the Authors) and one Director (the Editor) performing at a time. In true classic improv style, you can start the scene by asking for suggestions for subjects or setting. It doesn't really matter. You just need your actors to start talking to each other. You can always default to asking them to start acting out what they did the day before. Once they get going, the Director can shout out "Change it!" (or ring a bell, or honk a horn, or use any available audio cue). Then the Actor repeats the last sentence they said, changing the last word or phrase.

10. CROSSWORD WITH NAMES

Estimated time to play: 20 minutes
Supplies needed: Pens and paper, whiteboard
Ideal number of players: At least 4

How It Works

This is a two-part game. The first part is a simple icebreaker game that can be played in minutes. You can end it there or you can take it a step further and turn the game into a creative writing challenge.

Using either a whiteboard or a large sheet of paper, draw out a grid of 10 squares by 10 squares. Have each player take a turn writing their first name in the grid. Start at the top-left corner and write one letter per square. The next player starts in the next square and continues to the right. Do not leave any spaces blank. If you reach the end of a row, drop down to the next row and continue to write a letter in each square, starting all the way on the left. Once all players have written their names down, fill in any leftover squares with random letters. What you want in the end is a grid full of letters and no spaces. For smaller groups, you can make a smaller grid; for larger groups, enlarge the grid.

Now begins the word search. Give your players three to five minutes to write down as many words as they see in the grid. Boggle rules apply. Words can be formed by drawing a continuous invisible line from the first letter through the last letter, creating a letter chain. The letter chain may go in any direction (horizontally, vertically, diagonally, or zigzag) as long as the letters are adjacent.

Have your players read their list of words aloud. Whoever has the most words can be declared the winner, and you can stop right there. Or you can take the game a step further by challenging each player to write a poem or a short story that incorporates as many of the words as possible.

If you have a small group, you can play a variation of this game where you write down everyone's name without a grid and then all players try to form as many words as they can by simply scrambling the letters and rearranging any number of them in any manner they can think of.

11. ONE-SENTENCE SUMMARIES OR "BOY MEETS GIRL; DOESN'T END WELL FOR EITHER OF THEM."

Estimated time to play: 20 minutes
Supplies needed: Pens and paper
Ideal number of players: At least 3

How It Works

One-Sentence Summaries is a fun game to play with a group. It starts with just reading a list of one-sentence summaries of famous books and having players guess which books they are summarizing. A good one-sentence summary is totally accurate but somewhat vague. The example in the title "Boy Meets Girl; Doesn't End Well for Either of Them" could be the summary of several books, but in this specific case the correct answer is *Romeo and Juliet* by William Shakespeare. Once your players have heard several examples, give them a few minutes to write their own one-sentence summaries of books and have them read them out loud to the other players and have everyone guess the correct book.

One-sentence summaries are fun and easy to create. You can generate your own one-sentence summaries to use as examples. Try to pick books your group of players will actually know. Or, if you're lazy, you can just pick from the following list of examples:

Sample One-Sentence Summaries

A story of two brothers: one likes bunnies, the other one shoots him in the head: *Of Mice and Men* by John Steinbeck

The farm gets new management; the new management system is called horrible oppression: *Animal Farm* by George Orwell

A paleo diet with odd colors: *Green Eggs and Ham* by Dr. Seuss

This girl's pride makes her prejudiced against this dude, but they eventually work it out: *Pride and Prejudice* by Jane Austen

Dude hangs out by a small body of water and thinks the deep thoughts: *Walden* by Henry David Thoreau

Guy's wife disappears, doesn't look good for the guy, but then good news: the wife is a manipulative psychopath: *Gone Girl* by Gillian Flynn

Everybody is hungry, so kids kill each other for entertainment: *The Hunger Games* by Suzanne Collins

This bird reminds me of my dead wife: *The Raven* by Edgar Allan Poe

Boy takes advantage of a very generous plant: *The Giving Tree* by Shel Silverstein

After fighting in the Trojan War, this dude takes the long way home: *The Odyssey* by Homer

12. BAD BOOK TITLES OR "IMPERFECTIONS IN STRATOSPHERIC VISUAL PHENOMENON"

Estimated time to play: 20 minutes (or more)
Supplies needed: Pens and paper
Ideal number of players: At least 3

How It Works

The point of the game Bad Book Titles is to reimagine book titles. But instead of using creativity for good you are going to use it for evil in this game. You're going to make the book titles worse . . . or at the very least, much more cumbersome. The goal is to restate the title of the book as accurately as you can but by using the most obscure language possible. You can't add random words to the title but you can replace specific words with other language that means the same thing but is unnecessarily descriptive.

Much like One-Sentence Summaries, you start this game by reading several examples of Bad Book Titles. Your players will guess at the real book title. Once you have given enough examples, give your players a few minutes to write their own Bad Book Tiles. Have the players take turns reading them to everyone else and guessing at the original titles.

Bad Book Title Examples

A Frivolity of Plush Seats: *A Game of Thrones* by George R. R. Martin

That Gambling Game that You're More Likely to Get Struck by Lightning than Win: *The Lottery* by Shirley Jackson

The Lady Arachnid's Silky Abode: *Charlotte's Web* by E. B. White

The Devious Feline with Ornate Head Apparel: *The Cat in the Hat* by Dr. Seuss

The Giant Flaming Orb Will Too Ascend: *The Sun Also Rises* by Earnest Hemingway

Illegal Activity and the Judicial Repercussions: *Crime and Punishment* by Fyodor Dostoevsky

If you want to take the game further, you could have your players create new book covers with Bad Book Titles. You can make this game into a design and illustration project if you want. Don't hold back; go ahead and print off your new Bad Book Title covers and wrap library books with them. Make a special display of your "Re-Titled Books." Maybe circulation will go up for all the titles. You never know. Maybe they won't be such bad book titles after all.

13. GIBBERISH WITH DUBBING

Estimated time to play: 15 minutes
Supplies needed: None
Ideal number of players: 3–6

How It Works

This is an acting game that can be played with as few as three participants but not more than six at a time. If you have a large group, you can also take turns with six active players at a time.

To begin the game, select two to three actors to play out a scene. They can start acting out whatever they wish; the only rule is they cannot speak anything intelligible. They can, and should, speak gibberish, making emotive sounds but not saying anything that can be recognized as an actual language. Then one player for each actor plays the part of a voice actor dubbing the gibberish, by translating their lines into English. If you have a smaller group, you can also have one player dub all the lines of all the actors.

This is an interesting storytelling exercise because of the inherent tension between the gibberish actors trying to portray a story without words and the translators' interpretation of what they are doing. It is also usually very funny. This game is all about active listening and teamwork.

LONG GAMES (30+ MINUTES)

14. NAME THAT MOVIE

Estimated time to play: 30 minutes (or more)
Supplies needed: Pens and paper, whiteboard, internet access
Ideal number of players: At least 4

How It Works

This is fun game that starts as group brainstorming activity and turns into an individual creative writing exercise. To begin, explain to your group that you are going to create a movie. But instead of starting with a character, setting, or plot, you're going to build this movie around a soundtrack. Ask for suggestions for songs to use in the soundtrack. Write down all suggestions on a whiteboard or somewhere visible to all players. Players can suggest any song they would like. There doesn't have to be any kind of logic behind the song selection. Once you have a healthy list of song suggestions, with at least a dozen choices, vote on which songs you will use. Each player gets two votes. The two songs with the most votes win.

If you have the ability, play both songs either in their entirety or at least substantial clips of each. Do not watch music videos of the songs. Music videos can suggest narratives, and you don't want to hobble anyone's creativity with the suggestion of a preexisting narrative. The two songs you have selected are the soundtrack of your unnamed movie.

Brainstorm ideas for the title of the movie. Write down all title suggestions where they are visible to all players. Keep brainstorming until you have at least 20 movie titles. Take a vote. Players only get one vote this time. The title with the most votes becomes your official movie title.

All right. Now you have a soundtrack and a movie title. What's next? It's time to work on the preview, that's what. Using the movie title and the two songs in the soundtrack, each player must write the voice-over for a preview. For fun and inspiration, you can gather movie previews from the internet that feature prominent voice-over narration and play them as examples. Give your players 15 to 20 minutes to write their own voice-over narration for your fictional movie preview. You can also play the soundtrack songs in the background while players are writing their voice-overs. All players are working with the same movie title and soundtrack songs, but how they interpret those elements is completely up to them.

When your players are done writing, have them each read their movie preview voice-over in their best overly dramatic voice-over voice. If you wish, you can all vote on which fictional movie everyone wants to see the most. Give the winner a thematically appropriate prize, such as tickets to a movie theater or popcorn.

The game can end there or you can continue it as far as your players want to take. Making a movie poster is a great artistic and design challenge. Have players either draw the movie title lettering or use a computer to create a unique logo. A great free website, https://cooltext.com, can be used to generate fancy-looking logos in minutes. Have players illustrate the movie poster by collaging photos or creating original artwork and layering the movie title logo on top. You can also actually make a video of your preview. Use gathered still images to make a slideshow-style video. Or get out a video camera and have your teens film each other portraying the events in the movie. If you have access to a green screen, you can have all kinds of fun creating fantasy backgrounds. Put clips of your soundtrack in the movie and record the voice-over. Heck, if your teens are motivated enough, they could just go ahead and make the whole movie. Why not?

15. COMPLETE THE STORY

Estimated time to play: 30 minutes
Supplies needed: Pens and paper
Ideal number of players: At least 3

How It Works

This is a tried-and-true creative writing exercise that never fails to produce amusing results. The concept is simple: read a story, stop before you get to the ending, and then have your players write the ending to the story. Any story will work. But you will need to use a story that your players aren't already familiar with. For example, the three little pigs would not be a great story to use because everyone already knows the "real" ending to that story. Below is a sample story I've used many times for this exercise. It's a variation on a common ghost story that has many incarnations with differing setting and characters but the same simple plot. The most common version of this story is sometimes referred to as "The Phantom Hitchhiker." I call this version "Dearest John."

Dearest John, Part One

Once there was a wealthy farmer who owned a large estate that employed many laborers. This farmer was a widower who had one daughter whom he loved more than anything in whole world. Her name was Annette. The farmer was a jealous and possessive man and he had a strict rule that none of the laborers he employed on his farm were allowed to speak to his precious daughter. However, there was a handsome young laborer who worked on the farm named John who caught Annette's eye. She approached the young man in secret, and though he tried to resist, John succumbed to her charms. The two of them carried on in secret relationship, and soon the young couple fell hopelessly in love.

Then one day, unbeknown to Annette, John approached the farmer and asked for his daughter's hand in marriage. Outraged, the farmer accused John of betraying his trust and had him forcibly thrown off the farm. The farmer told John if he ever set eyes on him again, he would kill the young laborer.

Broken hearted, full of despair, and with nowhere to go, John walked away from the farm. He walked for miles and miles until the day turned to night. The frigid night sky loosed icy rain down upon John's weary body, chilling him to the bone. John collapsed on the road and died on the spot.

His body was found by strangers many miles from the farm. They did not recognize the boy, but they wanted to do right by his soul. So they said a blessing over his corpse and laid the body in an unmarked grave beside the road, topped with a smooth flat stone.

The next night, Annette awoke to knocking on the farmhouse door. She rose from her bed, wrapped a shawl around her shoulders, and went to the door. Annette released the latch and swung open the door. Standing on the doorstep was John. . . .

End of Dearest John, Part One

Give your participants 15 to 20 minutes to write what happens next. They can take the story wherever they wish, but they need to finish the story somehow. When they have finished, have them take turns reading the different endings to the story. This exercise is meant to be a celebration of creative diversity. Even given identical setups, each player will come up with an ending that is uniquely their own.

Inevitably, your participants will want to hear the "real" ending to the story. You can tell them their own endings are real and valid. Or you can just read them this:

Dearest John, Part Two

"John!" exclaimed Annette. "Where have you been? I haven't seen you all day."

John did not answer her. He had taken one of her father's horses from the stable, saddled it, and led it up to her door. "Let's go for a ride," he said.

They rode together without speaking, under the silent moon. Annette sat in the saddle behind John, her arms wrapped around him.

"John," she said, "you're so cold. Why are you so cold?"

John did not answer. Annette removed her shawl and wrapped it around John's shoulders. "Here," she said, "this will keep you warm."

When they returned to the farmhouse, John tried to return the shawl to Annette, but she refused. "You're still so cold, John. You keep it. I'll get it from you tomorrow."

She kissed John good night. His lips were like ice.

The next morning, Annette went looking for John, but she couldn't find him anywhere. She asked the farm laborers, but the last time anyone had seen John was two days ago walking away from the farm. Annette saddled a horse and started in the direction John was last seen walking.

After riding for some time, Annette came to an abrupt halt, her breath catching in her throat. There beside the road was a freshly dug grave with a smooth stone on top of it. Draped across the stone lay Annette's shawl.

16. CHARACTER BUILDING

Estimated time to play: 30 minutes
Supplies needed: Pens and paper
Ideal number of players: At least 3

How It Works

This is a group exercise where everyone works together to build a character. Have everyone sit in a circle. Select a player to go first. This player says one sentence that describes the character. The next person repeats the sentence and adds another sentence, further describing the character. The next player repeats the first two attribute and adds another sentence describing the character. It continues on in this fashion until everyone has contributed to the character description. If you have a smaller group, you can continue around the circle, each player contributing multiple details.

For example:

Player 1: This person is named Amanda.
Player 2: This person is named Amanda. Amanda only has one eye.
Player 3: This person is named Amanda. Amanda only has one eye. Amanda lost her eye fighting Nazis in World War II.

. . . And so on and so forth. Part of this exercise is listening to and recognizing what other people say. But players need not repeat everyone's sentence word for word. As long as they get the gist of the description, that's good enough.

Once you have a well-defined character, give your players 15 to 20 minutes to write a short story about the character. You could also have players draw a picture of the character or give them the choice of doing either.

17. THE STORY GAME

Estimated time to play: 30 minutes
Supplies needed: None
Ideal number of players: At least 4

How It Works

The Story Game is perhaps the greatest group storytelling creative exercise ever. There is one catch, though. It only works once. There is a trick to this game. And once you know the trick, you can never play it again.

This is how you play the Story Game. Select one to three players to be the "Guessers." Everyone else will be the "Storytellers." Instruct the Guessers that they must leave the room while the Storytellers concoct a story. When they return, they can ask yes or no questions to try and guess what the story is. Have the Guessers leave for a good 10 to 15 minutes to give ample time to create a story. Have them go for a walk or send them on a mission to buy ice cream. Just get them out of the room and doing something to occupy their time. Once the Guessers have departed and are far out of earshot, explain to the Storytellers that you are not going to make up a story. Instead, the Guessers will unintentionally create their own story with their questions.

When the Guessers return to the room, send them away again, saying you haven't quite finished the story yet and you need a few more minutes. You can keep sending them away if you wish, citing the need for more time. But don't be cruel and overdo it. When you've had enough time to pretend to make up a story, invite the Guessers back into the room. Explain again to the Guessers that they can only ask yes or no questions. And the only response the Storytellers are allowed to give is "Yes," "No," or "Sort of." If the guessers ask a question that is not a yes or no question, do not answer. Ask them to restate the question as a yes or no question.

The trick to this game is that any question the Guessers ask that ends with a word that ends with a consonant will be answered "no." Any question the Guessers ask that ends with a word that ends with a vowel will be answered "yes." Any question the Guessers ask that ends with the letter "y" will be answered with "Sort of." To help preserve the illusion of the game, it's a good idea for some of the Storytellers to answer questions that end with a "y" by at first saying "Yes" or "No" but then reconsidering and saying "Sort of."

This is an example of how a game might go:

Guessers:	Is this a fantasy story?
Storytellers:	Sort of.
Guessers:	Is it a fairy tale?
Storytellers:	Yes.
Guessers:	Does it have fairies in it?
Storytellers:	No.
Guessers:	Does it have a witch?
Storytellers:	No.
Guessers:	Does it have a wizard?
Storytellers:	No.
Guessers:	Does it have a princess?
Storytellers:	No.
Guessers:	Does it have a prince?
Storytellers:	Yes.
Guessers:	Was this prince brave?
Storytellers:	Yes.
Guessers:	Does the prince go on an adventure?
Storytellers:	Yes.

As the game goes on, periodically ask the Guessers to sum up what they know about the story so far. If the Guessers get frustrated, give them hints. Encourage them to keep at it. What you'll eventually end up with is the most bizarre, original story the Guessers don't even know they are writing themselves. The hard part of this game is knowing when to call it quits. You could go on forever and ever, but at some point you should decide that's enough and tell the Guessers they have figured out the entire story. Have them recap it one more time and reveal in the glory of its strangeness.

Once you are done, if you so choose, you can explain the trick to the Guessers and let them know they actually wrote the story themselves. The teaching moment being that everyone is capable of creating creative, bizarre, unique stories even if they don't realize they are making up the story as they guess. Alternatively, you can never tell the Guessers and keep playing the game forever—or until word eventually gets out and the Guessers learn the trick.

I once divided a teen group of 10 in half and had the five Guessers leave the room while I explained the trick of the game to the five Storytellers. After the Guessers finished "guessing" the story, we did not reveal the trick of the Storytelling Game to them. Instead, the Guessers insisted that they get a turn at making up a story. So the Storytellers and I left the room while they actually created a real story that we later had to piece together using yes or no questions. While we were outside the room and the other group was creating their story, we decided we would keep the secret of the trick to Story Game. And so we went on for months playing the Story Game with one group actually taking turns making up a story, while the other group just used the trick of the Story Game to trick the other group into unknowingly making up their own story with their questions. As far as I know, the one group of five teens still does not know the trick to the Story Game.

18. JAM COMIC

Estimated time to play: 60 minutes
Supplies needed: Pens and paper
Ideal number of players: At least 5

How It Works

Jam comics are a very straightforward creative collaboration game. They do require both writing and drawing. What they don't require is good writing or drawing. Participants just need to be willing to participate. Players sometimes get self-conscious about their artistic abilities in particular, but if you preface the game with an announcement that "stick figures are just fine," it will usually put players at ease.

To begin a jam comic, take a few pieces of paper and draw a grid of six squares (2 squares across and 3 squares down) for your panel layout on each page. Draw something in the first panel. Draw anything you like. It should be some sort of setup to a story. If you wish, add word balloons with dialogue or a caption box with narration. Then pass the page to the next player to continue the story by drawing and writing something in the next box. There is no restriction on what players write and draw as long as they progress the story in some fashion. Keep passing the pages around to each player. Players read the story thus far and then continue it by drawing and writing in the next panel.

Jam comics are fun because you never know where the story is going. The real trick to creating a successful jam comic is knowing when to stop. You can continue the game till you run out of paper. Then the burden of tying it up falls on the player who fills out the last blank panel. You'll likely end up with a more satisfying story if you give your players the freedom to end the story whenever they decide feels natural. When a player decides it's time to stop, simply have them write "The End" on their final panel. If you have excess blank panels, have the next player start a new story. If no one is willing to end the story, then it's your job as the game facilitator when your time is up to try and complete the story by adding one or two more panels to reach a satisfying ending.

When I begin a jam comic, I always try to make the drawing in the first panel extra crappy. This helps lower the bar for acceptable art and helps empower players who might be insecure about their drawing ability.

You can play a slight variation on this game where you simply pass a blank sheet of paper around the room and allow players to create their own panel shapes as they go. You'll get much more interesting page designs by playing this way, but I prefer using a simple grid. Jam comics always result in unexpected, bizarre story lines. Having panels laid out in a standard grid helps ground crazy stories in an easy-to-read format.

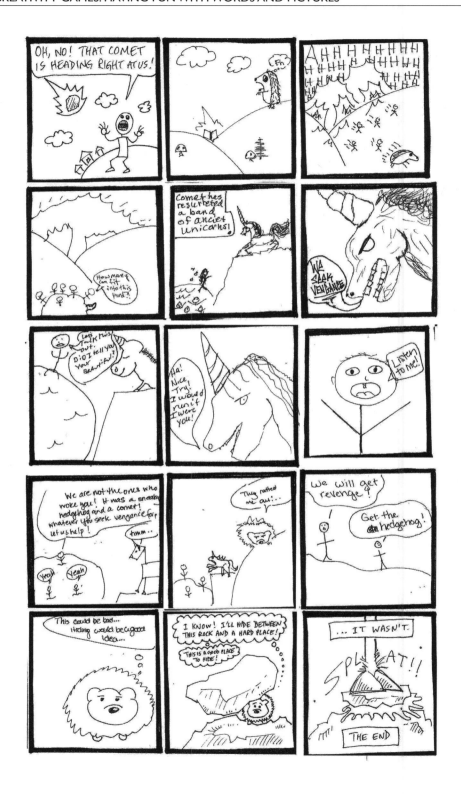

This is an example of a jam comic that got passed around the room during a graphic novel workshop I was running. I drew the first panel and then let it take on a life of its own. As is usual with jam comics, the story line progressed in a very unexpected way. At the end of the workshop, when the comic came back to me, it was not complete. So I did my best to tie up the story in the last two panels.

19. EXQUISITE CORPSE TELEPHONE PICTIONARY

Estimated time to play: 20 minutes (per round)
Supplies needed: Pens and paper
Ideal number of players: 6 or more

How It Works

All the games in this section are good creativity games. But this game is perhaps my favorite game of all time. Exquisite Corpse Telephone Pictionary combines both the writing and drawing versions of Exquisite Corpse with a game mechanic similar to the playground game Telephone to produce a game that is always hilarious.

To play the game, have your players seated around a table and pass out a piece of paper and a drawing implement to each player. All players should fold their papers into fourths, creating four rectangles. Have each player write a sentence in the top rectangle. It can really be anything, but I have found it useful to use some kind of creative writing prompt. My favorite prompt to use is "Write the first sentence of a book that you like or what you think would be a good first sentence for a book."

After each player has written a sentence, have them pass the paper to their right. Have each player read the sentence, and then in the next rectangle, have them interpret the sentence as best as they can in a quick drawing. It doesn't have to be a good drawing. Stick figures are fine. They are not allowed to write any words; it just has to be a drawing. Players are also not allowed to ask each other questions about the sentences or the drawings. They just have to interpret to the best of their ability. Give them a few minutes to complete their drawing and then have each player fold back the top rectangle so only the drawing is visible. Pass the papers to the right.

Now each player looks at the drawing and sum up in one sentence what they see in the drawing. Once everyone has written a sentence, have them fold the paper again so only the sentence is visible, and again pass to the right. The game proceeds this way with each player interpreting a sentence with a drawing and then a drawing with a sentence but only seeing what was in the rectangle right before. When players reach the fourth rectangle on the bottom of the page, have them flip the paper over and begin filling out the top rectangle on the backside of the paper. Once an image is drawn in the final rectangle at the bottom of the backside of the piece, have players fold the paper so only the last drawing is showing and pass to the right. The last step is to each player write one last sentence in the same rectangle as the final drawing, describing what they see in that drawing.

When players are done, they can unfold the papers and read the beautiful progression from the initial sentence to the final sentence. Have your players read the progression out loud to the group and show off the lovely illustrations. The object of this game is not to faithfully reproduce the same sentence and drawing over and

over but, rather, to marvel at where you can begin with an idea and where it can ultimately end up. The beauty and the humor of this game comes from the deviations and
misinterpretations. Creativity can come from making mistakes. Or to put it another
way, there are no mistakes in creativity games, just different ways of doing things.
Celebrate the differences.

20. WEREWOLF (A.K.A. MAFIA)

Estimated time to play: 30 minutes (or more)
Supplies needed: A deck of playing cards
Ideal number of players: 8 or more

How It Works

Werewolf is a party game for seven or more players, plus a narrator who moder-
ates the game but does not take an active role in the game play. This game combines
storytelling and acting with mob mentality to create a unique playing experience. The
setting of the game is a quaint, serene little village where life is ideal . . . until the sun
goes down and the moon rises. In the moonlight, certain Villagers transform into
bloodthirsty Werewolves and murder innocent Villagers in the black of night. When
the sun rises once again, everything returns to normal, except the village population
has been decreased by one. It is the goal of the Villagers to root out the werewolves
and exterminate them. It is the goal of the Werewolves to kill all the Villagers. The
trick is, no one knows who is just a Villager and who is really a Werewolf.

There are many, many versions of this game out there. But at the core, the game
play is the same. The group must work together to root out whatever hidden force
is murdering people in secret at night. Each night a villager is murdered (removed
from the game) and each day the village must make accusations and ultimately take a
vote on who they think is behind the murders and execute that player (remove them
from the game).

The original game was called Mafia and is said to have been invented in the Mos-
cow State University Psychology depart as a research project in the 1980s. The game
became popular at other Soviet schools and soon spread through Europe and then
into the United States. In the Mafia version of the game, at night, members of the
Mafia would murder a villager. During the day, the village would try and root out the
Mafia by executing a villager. The villains of the game were adapted from the Mafia to
Werewolves in the 1990s, and the Werewolf version of the game has become the most
popular way to play. But really any setting you can imagine can be used for this game.
The villains could be cannibals, aliens, vampires, witches, nocturnal zombies, demons, or
whatever you would like. For the mechanics of the game to make sense, the villains just
need to be able to disguise themselves as ordinary Villagers during the day. Other than
that, it's up to you how you want to play. Let your imagination run wild.

There are multiple board game and card game versions of Werewolf that can be
purchased. But all you really need is a deck of regular playing cards to play this game.
And in a pinch, scraps of paper with letters written on them work just as well. The
cards indicate players' roles in the game. A player's role is secret. It should never be
revealed to other players. A player can claim they have a certain role but they are not

allowed to show their card to anyone until they have "died" and then, and only then, does their role become public knowledge.

In a basic game of Werewolf, there are only two roles: Villagers and Werewolves. You can also play with "Special Villagers." Special Villagers have certain abilities than can be used at different times during the game to spice the game up a little. If you Google "Werewolf Rules" or "Mafia Rules," you will find countless Special Villager roles that can be used in the game. But if this is your first time playing Werewolf, I would recommend keeping it simple and just playing with Werewolves and Villagers. Below I list several Special Villager roles that can be used in place of regular Villager roles. As you get comfortable with the game, try introducing some Special Villager roles. But don't overdo it. A game with large group of people with lots and lots of Special Villager roles can become overly complicated and tiresome. A good rule of thumb is for half of the Villager roles in any given game to be regular Villagers and half can be Special Villagers.

To play the basic game, first decide who your Narrator will be. It is the Narrator's job to set the tone and facilitate the game, keeping things moving at a comfortable pace. The Narrator is a neutral party and is neither on the Villager nor on the Werewolf team. A typical game takes 10 to 20 minutes, so players can take turns taking on the role of the Narrator for different rounds if they wish. The Narrator takes a deck of cards and separates the red (hearts and diamonds) number cards and the black (clubs and spades) number cards. In a seven-person game, there should be five red number cards and two black number cards. Shuffle the cards and deal one, face down, to each player. Players may look at their cards but may not show them to anyone else. Players who received red number cards are Villagers. Players who received black number cards are Werewolves. If you are playing with a larger group, add in red cards for more Villagers. For every three Villagers you add, add one black number card for another Werewolf. So a game of 11 players would have three Werewolves, a game of 14 players would have four Werewolves, and so on.

Once each player has looked at their card, the Narrator begins the game. The following is a suggested game intro script. It can be modified as you see fit, as long as you keep the game playing mechanics intact. Part of the fun of this game is the storytelling aspect, and players should be encouraged to embellish whenever possible.

Game Introduction Script

Narrator: "Welcome to the village of [Insert Funny Name Here]. It's a quiet, quaint village, with good schools and affordable housing. The days are sunny and warm, and the nights are cool and pleasant. Life is easy in this village . . . At least it was, until a horrible plague of lycanthropy infested the town. Now there are Werewolves among us, stalking and murdering innocents at night. No one knows for sure who is a Werewolf and who is just a Villager. But desperate times call for desperate measures. It is up to you, the Villagers, to root out and execute the Werewolves before they overrun the town. Good luck."

After the introduction has been read, regular game play begins, with the Narrator describing events and instructing the players what to do next. Each round begins with the Narrator announcing that night has fallen.

Nightly Events Script and Player Instructions

Narrator: "The night has come and the sky is dark. All the Villagers have gone to sleep."

All players must close their eyes and put their heads down. Players should be silent (or as silent as possible) while asleep.

Narrator: "The full moon rises high in the inky black night. Werewolves awaken and acknowledge one another."

The players with the black number cards indicating that they are Werewolves open their eyes and raise their heads. Silently, the Werewolves look at one another and nod once they recognize each other.

Narrator: "Werewolves, choose your victim."

Gesturing silently, the Werewolves come to a consensus as to which villager they will murder.

Narrator: "Werewolves go to sleep."

The Werewolves close their eyes, lower their heads, and go back to sleep.

Narrator: "The sun has risen. It is a new day. All players, wake up."

All players lift their heads and open their eyes.

Narrator: "It's another beautiful day. However, not everyone gets to wake up today, because [Insert player name here] was viciously torn to shreds in the dead of night by Werewolves! It's a tragedy, but mourning will have to wait, because you only have until nightfall to root out the Werewolves among you and execute them before they murder you all in your sleep. Good luck."

The murdered player is now removed from the game. At this point they may show their card to all other players. They can remain present but they may not contribute to Villager discussions or execution votes. Murdered players may also stay awake with their eyes open when night falls again and observe nocturnal events. But murdered players must stay silent.

During daylight hours, living players may make accusations and debate among each other until they come to a consensus on who will be executed. Werewolves are Villagers also and they can and should participate in the debate. Of course, they need to be careful and not tip their hand and make it too obvious that they are Werewolves. Again, any player can claim a role, but no one is allowed to show their card until they are either murdered in the night by Werewolves or executed by the Villagers.

A player can make a formal accusation by saying, "I accuse [Player's Name] of being a Werewolf." If a second player seconds the accusation by stating, "I second the accusation!" it goes to a vote. All living Villagers participate in the vote. If a majority is achieved, the accused player is executed. It is up to the Narrator to describe the execution as grotesquely or as tastefully as they desire. Here is an example of a very grotesque narrated execution:

Execution Sample Script

Narrator: "I am very sorry, [Player's Name], but an angry mob of Villagers is convinced that you are in fact a Werewolf. The mob subdues you, binds your hands and legs, and lays your neck across a chopping block. The town butcher emerges from his fly-infested shop with his largest, sharpest meat cleaver in hand. He raises the blade aloft and holds it glimmering in the sun for a long moment before bringing it down with sickening 'Chop!' Your head rolls free from your body and bounces down the street, with a wet, soft splat, splat, splat . . . you . . . are . . . dead."

The executed player reveals their card to the other players who will rejoice if they successfully identified a Werewolf and removed them from the game or regret their poor decision if they unfortunately executed an innocent Villager.

Following the execution, night once again falls, and new round begins. The game progresses from night rounds to day rounds until either the Villagers have successfully executed all the Werewolves, in which case the Villagers win, or the Werewolves have murdered all the Villagers, in which case the Werewolves have won. It is the Narrator's job to stay impartial but to keep the game moving. If the Villagers are taking too long to decide whom to execute during the day, the Narrator may call for a vote at any time.

Special Villagers

Once you get the hang of the basic game, it can be fun to introduce Special Villagers into the role cards. Each Special Villager has an ability they can use at night (a few exceptions use their abilities during the daylight hours). When the Narrator is describing the events of the night, before the moon rises and the Werewolves choose their victim, the Narrator should ask each Special Villager to wake up one by one and ask them if and how they choose to use their special abilities (see the sample timeline below for a checklist of nighttime events). Players may choose to tell the other Villagers that they are special characters to stress their importance and dissuade other players for voting to execute them. Or Special Villagers may choose to keep their identities a secret so that they do not become targets of the Werewolves' nightly attacks. A player may not actually show their role card to anyone until they have died. To play with any Special Villager, replace a red number card with the red face card corresponding to the role listed below, before shuffling and distributing the roles at random. Again, there are many, many variations of Special Villagers that are used in different versions of the Werewolf game. A quick internet search will give you a long list of possibilities. What follows are the five most common Special Villagers.

List of Special Villagers
Ace of Hearts: The Doctor

The Doctor has the power of medicine on their side and they have the ability to heal a player who has been attacked by a Werewolf. When the Doctor awakes at night, the Narrator asks them if they wish to heal any player. The Doctor indicates which player they wish to heal by silently pointing to that player. The Doctor may choose to heal themselves. The Narrator nods to confirm they understand which player is being healed that night. Then the Doctor goes back to sleep. If the player who was selected to be healed that night is the same player whom the Werewolves choose to murder, that player is saved, and no one dies that night.

Ace of Diamonds: The Seer

The Seer has mystical abilities that allow them to gaze into their crystal ball at night and determine whether another player is a Werewolf or not. When the Seer awakes at night, the Narrator asks them to pick a person to determine if they are a Werewolf or not. The Seer silently indicates the player they choose, and the Narrator nods if that player is indeed a Werewolf or shakes their head if the player is a Villager.

Queen of Diamonds: The Witch

The Witch has two potions that can be used at night. One is a healing potion and the other is poison. Each potion can only be used once. When the Witch awakes at night, the Narrator asks if they wish to use their potions. The Witch nods or shakes their head. Then the Narrator asks who they wish to heal. The Witch silently indicates whom they wish to heal. And then the Narrator asks whom they wish to poison. The Witch then silently indicates whom they wish to poison. Each potion can only be used once throughout the game. If the player whom the Witch selected to be healed that night is the same player whom the Werewolves choose to murder, that player is saved, and no one dies that night. The player who is poisoned at night dies in addition to any player who is murdered by Werewolves that round. If the Doctor chooses to heal the same player whom the Witch poisons at night, that player does not die.

King of Hearts: The Hunter

The Hunter has a rifle. If the Hunter is executed by the Villagers, or murdered at night by the Werewolves, or poisoned by the Witch, the Hunter may fire their rifle and kill another player when they die. The Hunter may choose any living player to shoot. That player dies immediately and may not be saved by the Doctor or the Witch.

Jack of Hearts: The Insomniac

The Insomniac doesn't actually sleep at night. They only pretend to be asleep. When the moon rises, and the Werewolves wake up, the Insomniac may choose to peek and try and see who is a Werewolf. But if a Werewolf catches the Insomniac peeking, the Insomniac dies immediately in addition to whatever victim the Werewolves choose to attack that night. Werewolves will indicate they saw the Insomniac peeking to the Narrator by pointing at the Insomniac and bearing their teeth.

Gameplay Summary

1. All players go to sleep.
2. Werewolves wake up and choose their victim. Werewolves go back to sleep.
3. Narrator asks all Special Villagers to awake one by one and asks them if they wish to use their special abilities before going back to sleep:
   a. Doctor
   b. Seer
   c. Witch
4. All players wake up.
5. Murdered victims are announced.
6. Villagers debate and vote to execute a player.
7. Night begins again . . .

CHAPTER TWO

GRAPHIC NOVEL CREATION

COMICS ARE A TERRIFIC MEDIUM FOR CREATIVE EXPRESSION. THEY'RE EASILY ACCESSIBLE AND, UNLIKE A MOVIE OR A PLAY, A SINGLE PERSON CAN CREATE A FINISHED PRODUCT ON THEIR OWN, WITH NOTHING MORE THAN A PEN OR A PENCIL AND PIECE OF PAPER, MAKING IT A VERY PERSONAL ARTISTIC STATEMENT.

COMICS CAN EMPOWER YOUNG PEOPLE TO TELL WHATEVER KINDS OF STORIES THEY CHOOSE. IF YOU'RE GOING TO TEACH A WORKSHOP ON HOW TO MAKE GRAPHIC NOVELS WITH TEENS, YOU DON'T NECESSARILY HAVE TO MAKE COMICS YOURSELF OR BE ANY SORT OF ARTIST. BUT YOU DO NEED TO UNDERSTAND HOW COMICS WORK.

THE GOOD NEWS IS, IF YOU READ GRAPHIC NOVELS, YOU MOST LIKELY ALREADY UNDERSTAND THIS STUFF INNATELY, BUT MAY NOT HAVE THE CONFIDENCE OR VOCABULARY TO EXPLAIN IT PROPERLY. IN THIS SECTION OF THE BOOK, WE'RE GOING TO BREAK DOWN THE MEDIUM, EXPLAIN HOW IT ALL WORKS, AND POINT OUT SOME OF THE PITFALLS NEW COMICS CREATORS OFTEN FALL INTO.

From *Murder Mystery, Graphic Novels, and More: Innovative Programs for Engaging Teens in Your Library* by Thane Benson. Santa Barbara, CA: Libraries Unlimited. Copyright © 2019.

THERE ARE TWO IMPORTANT THINGS WORTH NOTING ABOUT THE INTRODUCTION OF NEWSPAPER COMICS. FIRST, THAT THEY WERE IMMEDIATELY EXTREMELY POPULAR WITH THE PUBLIC, LARGELY DUE TO THE ACCESSIBILITY OF THE MEDIUM.

WE LOVE COMICS!

AND SECONDLY, THAT THE ART FORM WAS BELITTLED BY HIGH SOCIETY FOR THE EXACT SAME REASON.

THIS ISN'T ART! ART HANGS IN A MUSEUM WHERE THE COMMON FOLK CAN'T GET THEIR GRUBBY LITTLE FINGERS ON IT.

COMICS' REPUTATION OF BEING SUB-LITERATE TRASH CLUNG TO THE MEDIUM AS COMIC STRIPS WERE COLLECTED AND PRINTED INTO MAGAZINES THAT BECAME KNOWN AS COMIC BOOKS.

OF COURSE, IT DOESN'T HELP THAT SOME COMICS ARE NOT VERY GOOD. BUT, IN ALL FAIRNESS, NOT EVERYTHING THAT GETS HUNG IN A MUSEUM IS NECESSARILY GOOD EITHER.

HEY, MISTER! WHAT MAKES THAT ART?

WHAT IS ART ANYWAY?

FINE ART

BECAUSE I SAID SO! THAT'S WHY!

IN THE 1970s THE TERM "GRAPHIC NOVEL" BEGAN TO BE USED LARGELY AS A MARKETING PLOY.

I CAN'T HAVE THIS COMIC BOOK GARBAGE IN MY RESPECTABLE BOOK STORE.

OH, BUT THIS ISN'T A COMIC BOOK. IT'S A... A... A GRAPHIC NOVEL!

OH! IN THAT CASE, I'LL BUY 50! NO, 100 COPIES!

BIG COMIC BOOK

WE ♥ BOOKS BUT NOT COMICS

SNAKE OIL

MR. SALESMAN

TODAY, GRAPHIC NOVEL SECTIONS ARE COMMONPLACE IN BOOKSTORES AND LIBRARIES, NEITHER OF WHICH WOULD HAVE EVER CONSIDERED PUTTING "COMIC BOOKS" ON THEIR SHELVES 20 YEARS AGO.

AND WHILE I'M THRILLED THAT THE MEDIUM HAS GAINED SO MUCH MORE CREDIBILITY IN THE PUBLIC EYE, IT'S TROUBLING TO ME THAT IT TOOK A NAME CHANGE TO MAKE THAT HAPPEN.

THE PROBLEM IS WHEN PEOPLE EQUATE THE TERM "GRAPHIC NOVEL" WITH A LEGITIMATE WORK OF ART AND CONTINUE TO ASSOCIATE THE TERM "COMICS" WITH SUB-LITERATE TRASH.

From *Murder Mystery, Graphic Novels, and More: Innovative Programs for Engaging Teens in Your Library* by Thane Benson. Santa Barbara, CA: Libraries Unlimited. Copyright © 2019.

YOU CAN ARGUE THAT GRAPHIC NOVELS TEND TO BE LONGER WORKS THAN COMIC BOOKS. GRAPHIC NOVELS ALSO TEND TO BE PUBLISHED IN A FANCIER FORMAT WITH A SPINE, LIKE A PROPER BOOK. WHEREAS COMICS ARE FLOPPY THINGS WITH STAPLES IN THEM MORE AKIN TO A MAGAZINE THAN A BOOK.

ANOTHER DISTINCTION SOME PEOPLE DRAW IS THAT A GRAPHIC NOVEL IS A COMPLETE STORY, WHEREAS A COMIC BOOK IS A PIECE OF A SERIALIZED STORY. BUT TO EQUATE A PUBLISHING FORMAT WITH QUALITY IS LUDICROUS (TALK ABOUT JUDGING A BOOK BY ITS COVER).

FURTHERMORE, SOME GRAPHIC NOVELS TELL STORIES ACROSS MULTIPLE VOLUMES, WHEREAS SOME SINGLE- ISSUE COMIC BOOKS TELL COMPLETE STORIES IN THEMSELVES. AND LET US NOT FORGET, SOME OF THE MOST CELEBRATED GRAPHIC NOVELS OF ALL TIME (SUCH AS MAUS AND WATCHMEN, TO NAME JUST TWO) WERE ORIGINALLY PUBLISHED AS SERIALIZED FLOPPY COMICS. SO WHAT'S THE DIFFERENCE, REALLY?

I USE THE TERMS "GRAPHIC NOVEL" AND COMICS" INTERCHANGEABLY.

SO THERE!

HA!

NOW THAT WE GOT THAT ELEPHANT OUT OF THE WAY, LET'S TALK ABOUT THE TERMINOLOGY AND MECHANICS OF COMICS (AND GRAPHIC NOVELS).

THE ACCESSIBILITY OF COMICS, AS I'VE MENTIONED SEVERAL TIMES ALREADY, IS ONE OF THE MEDIUM'S GREATEST STRENGTHS. ITS STRENGTH IS TWO-FOLD. COMICS ARE ACCESSIBLE BECAUSE THEY ARE EASY TO READ AND THEY ARE DOUBLY ACCESSIBLE BECAUSE THEY ARE MASS-PRODUCED AND DISTRIBUTED TO THEIR AUDIENCE.

INNOVATIONS IN PRINTING TECHNOLOGY HAVE MADE SHORT-RUN PRINTING EASIER AND MORE INEXPENSIVE THAN EVER BEFORE. TODAY, YOU CAN PRINT A SINGLE ISSUE OF A COMIC BOOK FOR A FEW DOLLARS.

WE CAN REBUILD HIM. WE HAVE THE TECHNOLOGY. WE CAN MAKE HIM BETTER THAN HE WAS. BETTER... STRONGER... FASTER...

YES, MASTER.

TRADITIONAL COMICS ARE PRINTED ON PAPER. IF YOU'RE GOING TO PRINT YOUR COMICS, WHICH YOU ABSOLUTELY SHOULD, YOU NEED TO UNDERSTAND SOME BASIC PRINTING TERMINOLOGY.

THE PAGE IS EXACTLY WHAT IT SOUNDS LIKE; IT'S THE PAGE OF A PRINTED BOOK.

TWO PAGES FACING EACH OTHER ARE REFERRED TO AS A DOUBLE-PAGE SPREAD.

DOUBLE-PAGE SPREADS ALWAYS START WITH AN EVEN-NUMBERED PAGE ON THE LEFT AND AN ODD- NUMBERED PAGE ON THE RIGHT. THE VERY BOOK YOU ARE HOLDING RIGHT NOW IS NO EXCEPTION. IF YOU FLIPPED THROUGH THIS BOOK, YOU WOULD SEE THAT THE EVEN-NUMBERED PAGES ARE ALWAYS ON THE LEFT AND ODD NUMBERS ARE ALWAYS ON THE RIGHT.

THIS IS A RULE. ALL BOOKS ARE FORMATTED THAT WAY (UNLESS AN INSANE PERSON IS NUMBERING THE PAGES). THIS IS SOMETHING THAT YOU NEED TO KEEP IN MIND AS YOU PLAN OUT YOUR COMIC, IN CASE YOU WANT TO GET FANCY AND HAVE SOME IMAGES THAT CROSS OVER A DOUBLE- PAGE SPREAD. IF YOU WANT TO GET REAL FANCY, YOU CAN PACE OUT YOUR COMIC TO KNOW WHEN A PAGE TURN IS HAPPENING AND USE THAT FOR DRAMATIC EFFECT (WE'LL TALK MORE ABOUT THIS LATER).

From *Murder Mystery, Graphic Novels, and More: Innovative Programs for Engaging Teens in Your Library* by Thane Benson. Santa Barbara, CA: Libraries Unlimited. Copyright © 2019.

IF YOU'RE GOING TO DESIGN YOUR OWN COMIC (OR GRAPHIC NOVEL), OR HELP SOMEONE DESIGN THEIR OWN COMIC (OR GRAPHIC NOVEL), YOU NEED TO UNDERSTAND A LITTLE BIT ABOUT PRINT LAYOUT. BELOW IS AN EXAMPLE OF A PRE-PRESS DOUBLE-PAGE SPREAD WITH DIFFERENT SECTIONS FILLED IN WITH SOLID BLACK AND GRAY FOR CLARITY. ON A REGULAR PRE-PRESS PAGE LAYOUT, THESE AREAS WOULD BE LEFT BLANK.

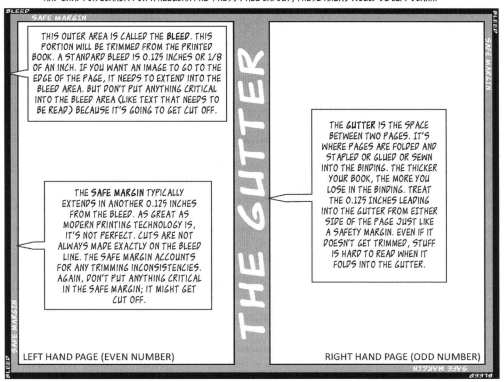

From *Murder Mystery, Graphic Novels, and More: Innovative Programs for Engaging Teens in Your Library* by Thane Benson. Santa Barbara, CA: Libraries Unlimited. Copyright © 2019.

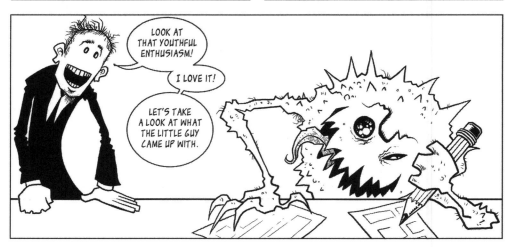

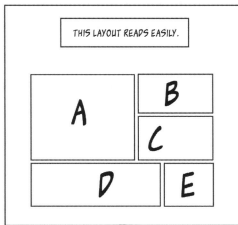

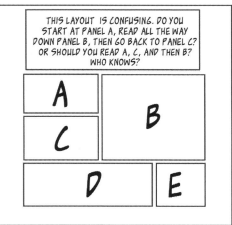

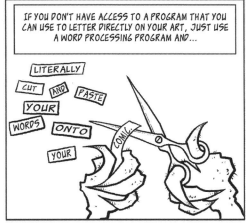

From *Murder Mystery, Graphic Novels, and More: Innovative Programs for Engaging Teens in Your Library* by Thane Benson. Santa Barbara, CA: Libraries Unlimited. Copyright © 2019.

HERE'S AN EXAMPLE OF A PLOT-STYLE SCRIPT.

THIS PLOT SCRIPT WOULD THEN BE GIVEN TO AN ARTIST WHO WOULD BE RESPONSIBLE FOR BREAKING DOWN THE STORY PAGE BY PAGE AND PANEL BY PANEL. ONCE THE COMIC WAS DRAWN, IT WOULD BE HANDED BACK TO THE WRITER, WHO WOULD THEN BE RESPONSIBLE FOR ADDING IN THE DIALOGUE AS WELL AS ANY NARRATION.

PLOT-STYLE SCRIPTS GIVE THE ARTIST A LOT OF FREEDOM TO PACE THE STORY AS THEY SEE FIT. IT ALSO PUTS THE RESPONSIBILITY FOR TELLING THE STORY VISUALLY SQUARELY ON THE SHOULDERS OF THE ARTIST.

PLOT:

The Extraordinary Adventures of Linda Splitz, Court Stenographer.

7-page short story comic

Linda Splitz is a court stenographer in New York City. She hates her job. It's really boring. One day while transcribing a monotonous traffic violation trial, an alien spaceship crashes through the roof of the courthouse. Hostile aliens emerge from the ship and attack. Linda Splitz, armed only with her typewriter, fights off the aliens. The aliens, hopelessly outmatched, flee.

Later, Linda Splitz recalls the event for reporters. During the interview she is again attacked by aliens. This time they've come armed with a giant robot, custom-built to destroy earth's most powerful defender: Linda Splitz, Court Stenographer.

An epic battle ensues that's very exciting and incredibly dramatic and stuff. But ultimately, Linda wins! New York City throws a parade in her honor. A week later, she's back in court, transcribing another really boring trial.

The End.

The Extraordinary Adventures of Linda Splitz, Court Stenographer.

7-page short story comic

PAGE 1

Panel 1.
Close-up of a woman's face, looking directly at the camera over her horn-rimmed glasses. She is bored out of her mind. Her eyes are glazed over, almost zombie-like. This is LINDA SPLITZ, our protagonist. She's a woman in her late 30s, very fit but not overly muscular. She eats well and runs a lot but doesn't lift weights. She is dressed in a conservative, professional manner. Her hair is done up tightly but just a few wisps are coming loose.

CAPTION (1):
I hate my life.

Panel 2.
Wider view. We can see LINDA SPLITZ is typing away at her typewriter in her little box next to the judge in a courtroom. The judge is a stereotypical stuffy old white man in a black robe. In the foreground, a bland lawyer in a bland suit is reading from a transcript for a jury. It is a typical courtroom scene. Nothing exciting or interesting is happening.

CAPTION (1):
Being a court stenographer is the most boring job in the world.

CAPTION (2):
The movies make trials look exciting.

FULL-SCRIPT WRITING MORE CLOSELY RESEMBLES SCREENPLAY WRITING.

BUT UNLIKE SCREENPLAY WRITING, THERE IS NO STANDARD FORMAT.

THAT BEING SAID, MOST COMIC BOOK AND GRAPHIC NOVEL FULL SCRIPT MANUSCRIPTS WILL LOOK SOMETHING SIMILAR TO THIS EXAMPLE.

THIS IS A 7-PAGE SHORT STORY. A STANDARD COMIC BOOK YOU'D FIND ON A NEWS-STAND IS 24 PAGES LONG (ALTHOUGH IT CAN CONTAIN SEVERAL SHORT STORIES).

GRAPHIC NOVELS USUALLY START AT 48 PAGES AND GO UP FROM THERE.

From *Murder Mystery, Graphic Novels, and More: Innovative Programs for Engaging Teens in Your Library* by Thane Benson. Santa Barbara, CA: Libraries Unlimited. Copyright © 2019.

PAGE 1 (Continued)

CAPTION (3):
Trials are not exciting.

CAPTION (4):
Trials are long. Trials are repetitive.
Trials are monotonous.

Panel 3.
Close-up of LINDA SPLITZ'S hands on the
typewriter keys. A portion of the court
transcript she is typing out is visible
and easy to read. It's okay if the captions
cover some of the transcript.

COURT TRANSCRIPT READS:
Blah, Blah, Blah, Blibbity-Blah, Blah…

CAPTION (1):
And it's my job to transcribe

CAPTION (2):
every

CAPTION (3):
single

CAPTION (4):
word.

Panel 4.
LINDA SPLITZ faces the camera
squarely. Her hands are in the foreground
typing away at the keys. She is bored,
bored, bored.

CAPTION (1)
Sometimes it gets so bad, I accidentally
start typing my interior dialogue.

Panel 5.
Close-up of hands typing on typewriter
with text on page clearly visible.

COURT TRANSCRIPT READS:
Blah Blah Blah Blah Blah Blah
I HATE MY LIFE Blah Blah Blah
THIS IS SO BORING Blah Blah Blah
I WISH SOMETHING EXCITING WOULD HAP-

Panel 6.
Extreme close-up of LINDA SPLITZ looking
up in surprise.

LINDA SPLITZ (1):
What the--?!!

PAGE 2 (3 panels)

Panel 1.
An enormous alien spaceship comes crash-
ing through the ceiling of the courthouse.
The ship is sleek and futuristic with all
kinds of wires and cogs and stuff showing. It is clearly not of this world. People
dive everywhere for cover. LINDA SPLITZ
is surprised but not fearful. She stands
in the foreground in a defiant, heroic
pose. There is chaos all around her. LINDA
SPLITZ holds her typewriter in hand. The
words "What the--?!!" are clearly visible,
typed out on the sheet still loaded into
the typewriter.

Panel 2.
Three aliens in futuristic combat gear,
armed with laser cannons, emerge from the
ship. These are typical "little green men"
aliens- sort of silly looking. But their
battle suits are very ominous and threatening. Their expressions are grim. One
alien, clearly the leader of this little
army, stands in the foreground.

ALIEN LEADER (1)
Attention, earthlings. This is a hostile
alien takeover. We have decided to annex
your planet.

PAGE 2 (Continued)

Panel 3
Close-up of ALIEN LEADER. He looks very intimidating and sadistic, like a cross between Genghis Khan and Hannibal Lecter.

ALIEN LEADER (1)
Submit now or face total annihilation.

PAGE 3 (7 panels)

Panel 1
Close-up of ALIEN LEADER looking to his right. A shadow is cast over him. He's looking worried. LINDA SPLITZ, unseen, is yelling from off-panel.

LINDA SPLITZ (off panel) (1)
Not on my watch, buckaroo!

ALIEN LEADER (2)
Huh?

Panel 2
LINDA SPLITZ clocks the ALIEN LEADER over the head with her typewriter. There's a loud noise followed by the ding of the typewriter. ALIEN LEADER spits out a tooth.

SFX (1)
KA-WHAM!

SFX (2)
Ding!

ALIEN LEADER (3)
Ooof!

Panel 3
ALIEN TWO raises his cannon to shoot.

ALIEN TWO (1)
How dare you stike our beloved commander! Die, insolent earth-scum—

Panel 3
LINDA SPLITZ throws her typewriter from off panel into the frame where it strikes ALIEN TWO in the head, knocking him unconscious before he has a chance to fire. Again, there's a loud noise followed by the ding of the typewriter.

SFX (1)
SHHHH-CLUNK

SFX (2)
Ding!

Panel 4
LINDA SPLITZ jumps into the air, with a very impressive freeze-frame pose reminiscent of the Matrix movies. She holds a stapler in one hand, cocked back and ready to strike. The last alien standing, ALIEN THREE, is desperately blasting away with his flame thrower, but is missing.

SFX (1)
FOOSH!

Panel 5
Close-up of the stapler being pressed against ALIEN THREE, firing a staple into his forehead. It hurts. A lot. ALIEN THREE screams in pain.

SFX (1)
CHA-CHUNK!

ALIEN THREE (2)
Yeeee-Owch!

Panel 6
All three aliens flee, running up the gangplank back into their spaceship. They've had enough. LINDA SPLITZ stands defiant, hands on hips, giving a stern, disapproving look at the aliens as they run away.

PAGE 4 (7 panels)

Panel 1
The panel border is a TV screen. An on-the-scene reporter is making an energetic live report into the camera. The destroyed courthouse is visible in the background.

TV REPORTER (1)
We're here on the scene at the city court-house, where just moments ago a hostile alien force attempted to launch an inva-sion to take over the planet Earth.

Panel 2
The TV screen shows the TV REPORTER grabbing a stunned LINDA SPLITZ by the arm and hauling her in front of the camera for an impromptu interview. LINDA SPLITZ doesn't know what to say.

TV REPORTER (1)
We've just learned that this would-be in-vasion of our planet was single-handedly thwarted by one brave woman. Tell us, who are you?

LINDA SPLITZ (2)
uh…

Panel 3
TV screen showing a close-up of LINDA SPLITZ, still dazed.

LINDA SPLITZ (1)
…Hi.
I'm Linda Splitz…
Court Stenographer.

Panel 4
Outer Space. A galactic armada of alien spaceships float in a sea of planets and stars. The flagship of the alien armada is at the forefront. It is much larger than the other ships.

CAPTION (1)
Meanwhile, poised just on the edge of the solar system, an invasion armada lies in wait…

Panel 5
The interior of the flagship. Two aliens are hunched over a screen. These are ALIEN GENERALS. They are battle-hardened, grizzled old warhorses. They have scars and are smoking cigars. They're tough. But they are also little green men and kind of silly looking. On the screen is the same TV image of LINDA SPLITZ. They have intercepted the earth broadcast.

LINDA SPLITZ (on the TV) (1)
…Hi.
I'm Linda Splitz…
Court Stenographer.

ALIEN GENERAL ONE (2)
So… this is earth's mightiest defender.

ALIEN GENERAL TWO (3)
The only thing between us and total global domination.

Panel 5
Close-up of ALIEN GENERAL ONE looking grim.

ALIEN GENERAL ONE (1)
We're not taking any more chances. Launch the R.O.P.O.D.!

Panel 6
ALIEN GENERAL TWO is shocked and alarmed at the order. ALIEN GENERAL ONE remains steadfast.

ALIEN GENERAL TWO (1)
But, General… Don't you think that's over-kill? The last time we used the R.O.P.O.D. it nuked half a solar system. Earth is no good to us if we blow it up.

PAGE 4 (Continued)

REPORTER (on the TV) (2)
So tell us, Ms. Splitz, what exactly does a court stenographer do?

LINDA SPLITZ (on the TV) (3)
Uh, well…

Panel 7
Close-up of ALIEN GENERAL ONE.

ALIEN GENERAL ONE (1)
Desperate times call for desperate measures. It's time to bring out the big guns. Linda Splitz will never know what hit her.

Page 5 (8 panels)

Panel 1
LINDA SPLITZ is finishing describing her job to the REPORTER. The REPORTER is disgusted with how boring LINDA SPLITZ's job is. We can see the CAMERA MAN standing behind her, with the courthouse ruins all around.

CAPTION (1)
Minutes later, back on earth…

LINDA SPLITZ (2)
…And that's pretty much what I do… Everyday.

REPORTER (3)
Wow… that's… really boring.

LINDA SPLITZ (4)
Tell me about it.

Panel 2
The CAMERA MAN whips his camera up to film a rocket barreling down out of the sky headed straight for them. LINDA SPLITZ and the REPORTER look up in alarm.

CAMERA MAN (1)
Whoah! Take a look at that!

Panel 3
LINDA SPLITZ dives out of the way, pushing the CAMERA MAN and the REPORTER to safety while the rocket slams down into the ground behind them in an explosion of debris flying everywhere.

LINDA SPLITZ (1)
Look out!

Panel 4 – 7: 4-panel progression
The rocket transforms into a giant robot, the R.O.P.O.D. It's huge and menacing with one evil red eye right in the middle. It's got lasers and rockets and chainsaws and all kinds of crazy, over-the-top weaponry. It speaks in a squawky computerized voice that overlays all three panels. Its word balloons should be hard angled and use an old-school computerized font for the lettering.

R.O.P.O.D. (1)
>:[Linda Splitz! Prepare… to be… eradicated!

Panel 8
LINDA SPLITZ leaps into action, jumping at the camera. She's not scared. She's pretty angry. You might even say she's pissed off at this point, although she would never resort to such lurid language. In the background, the REPORTER and the CAMERA MAN look on in astonishment. The CAMERA MAN is looking through the viewfinder of his camera.

LINDA SPLITZ (1)
That's it! I have had enough alien invasions for today! And I am not going to tolerate any more!

PAGE 5 (Continued)

REPORTER (to CAMERA MAN) (2)
Are you getting this?
Are you getting this?

CAMERA MAN (3)
I'm getting it!

R.O.P.O.D. (4)
>:0 Die, human scum!

LINDA SPLITZ (5)
Oh, put a sock in it, why don't you?!!

PAGE 6 (6 panels)

Panel 1.
Steel cable tentacles wrap around LINDA SPLITZ, suspending her, trapped, in mid-air. LINDA SPLITZ struggles and grimaces with the effort but cannot break free. The R.O.P.O.D. looms over her, ready for the kill, the one robotic eye glaring evilly.

R.O.P.O.D. (1)
>:P You fight bravely, but your cause is hopeless.
}:) Any last words before you are terminated?

LINDA SPLITZ (2)
Yeah... What's that in your eye?

Panel 2.
Close-up of LINDA SPLITZ's hand. She's managed to wriggle free one arm. In her hand she holds a small bottle clearly labeled as "White-Out." She is popping the cap off with her thumb.

Panel 3.
Close-up of LINDA SPLITZ flinging White-Out into the R.O.P.O.D.'s eye, blinding it.

SFX (1)
Splat!

R.O.P.O.D. (2)
<:/ ?

Panel 4.
The R.O.P.O.D. recoils in surprise and horror at being blinded. It releases LINDA SPLITZ, who drops to the ground gracefully like a cat, or a ninja, or maybe a ninja cat. At her feet is her trusty typewriter, a little banged up but still serviceable.

R.O.P.O.D. (1)
D:< I cannot see! What have you done?!! D:<

LINDA SPLITZ (2)
I'm only going to say this one more time. So listen up...

Panel 5.
LINDA SPLITZ holds her typewriter over head, poised to throw it.

LINDA SPLITZ (1)
...As long as I'm standing here, drawing breath, the earth isn't yours for the taking.

Panel 6.
LINDA SPLITZ throws the typewriter; it goes through the R.O.P.O.D., causing an explosion with a large "Boom!" sound effect and a little "Ding!" of the typewriter bell. The people cheer and celebrate this great victory for humanity.

LINDA SPLITZ (1)
Not today. Not ever!

SFX (2)
Ka-Boom!

SFX (3)
Ding!

R.O.P.O.D. (4)
:-0

PAGE 7 (6 Panels)

Panel 1
Outer Space. The galactic armada of alien spaceships still floats in a sea of stars.

Panel 2.
Inside the Alien Flagship the two alien Generals look at their monitor screen. It shows the last panel from the previous page, LINDA SPLITZ throwing the type-writer through the R.O.P.O.D., causing an explosion.

LINDA SPLITZ (on screen) (1)
...Not ever!

Panel 3.
Close-up of ALIEN GENERAL ONE looking bitter. His words come out begrudgingly.

ALIEN GENERAL ONE (2)
Give the order to withdraw the attack armada. This... court stenographer is more than we bargained for...

Panel 4.
The panel border is a TV screen. The REPORTER is interviewing LINDA SPLITZ again.

REPORTER (1)
Tell us, Ms. Splitz! How does it feel to save the human race twice in one day?

LINDA SPLITZ (2)
I... I...

The TV screen shows a close-up of LINDA SPLITZ smiling for the first time.

LINDA SPLITZ (1)
...I'm just happy I didn't have to transcribe the whole thing...

Panel 5.
LINDA SPLITZ is crumbled in despair, her face pressed against her little desk in the courtroom as she types. A faceless lawyer is blabbering on. Everything is back to the way it was. Typed clearly on the paper in her typewriter is a note that reads: "I hate my life."

CAPTION (1)
Two weeks later...

LAWYER (2)
Blah, Blah, Blah...

CAPTION (3)
The End

AS YOU CAN SEE, FULL SCRIPT WRITING IS MUCH MORE DENSE. NOTE THAT EACH PAGE IS DEFINED BY PAGE NUMBER AND THE NUMBER OF PANELS IN EACH PAGE. ALL DIALOGUE, CAPTIONS, AND SOUND EFFECTS WITHIN EACH PANEL HAVE AN ASSIGNED NUMBER SHOWING THE ORDER THAT THEY SHOULD BE READ IN.

THE STORY IS DESCRIBED BEAT BY BEAT IN DETAIL. EACH PAGE IS DESCRIBED SEPARATELY, AS IS EACH PANEL. THE PAGE BREAKS IN THE STORY ARE VERY DELIBERATE AND ARE USED TO BUILD TENSION. FOR EX-AMPLE, PAGE ONE ENDS WITH A CLOSE UP OF LINDA SPLITZ'S SURPRISED REACTION TO SOMETHING. BUT THE READER MUST TURN TO PAGE 2 TO SEE THAT IT IS ALIENS THAT HAVE CRASHED INTO THE COURTHOUSE.

IF YOU'RE WRITING FOR ANOTHER ARTIST, YOU WANT TO GIVE AS MUCH INFORMATION AS POSSIBLE TO HELP SET THE SCENE. EVEN IF YOU ARE WRITING FOR YOURSELF, IT CAN ONLY HELP TO SUPPLY AS MANY DETAILS AS POSSIBLE.

DETAILS THAT WON'T EVEN MAKE IT INTO THE FINAL COMIC OR GRAPHIC NOVEL ARE STILL VALUABLE TO GIVE A SENSE OF CHARACTER OR SETTING TO INFORM THE DRAWING.

From *Murder Mystery, Graphic Novels, and More: Innovative Programs for Engaging Teens in Your Library* by Thane Benson. Santa Barbara, CA: Libraries Unlimited. Copyright © 2019.

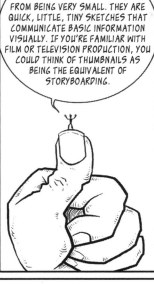

From *Murder Mystery, Graphic Novels, and More: Innovative Programs for Engaging Teens in Your Library* by Thane Benson. Santa Barbara, CA: Libraries Unlimited. Copyright © 2019.

From *Murder Mystery, Graphic Novels, and More: Innovative Programs for Engaging Teens in Your Library* by Thane Benson.
Santa Barbara, CA: Libraries Unlimited. Copyright © 2019.

"WE'RE HERE ON THE SCENE AT THE CITY COURTHOUSE, WHERE JUST MOMENTS AGO A HOSTILE ALIEN FORCE ATTEMPTED TO LAUNCH AN INVASION TO TAKE OVER THE PLANET EARTH. BUT NOW IT APPEARS THE ALIENS ARE RETREATING."

"WE'VE JUST LEARNED THAT THIS WOULD-BE INVASION OF OUR PLANET WAS SINGLE-HANDEDLY THWARTED BY ONE BRAVE WOMAN. TELL US, WHO ARE YOU?"

"UH..."

"...HI.

I'M LINDA SPLITZ...

COURT STENOGRAPHER."

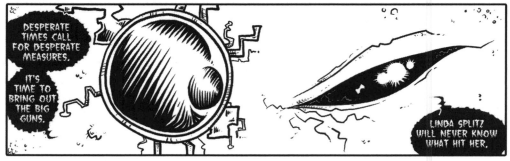

From *Murder Mystery, Graphic Novels, and More: Innovative Programs for Engaging Teens in Your Library* by Thane Benson. Santa Barbara, CA: Libraries Unlimited. Copyright © 2019.

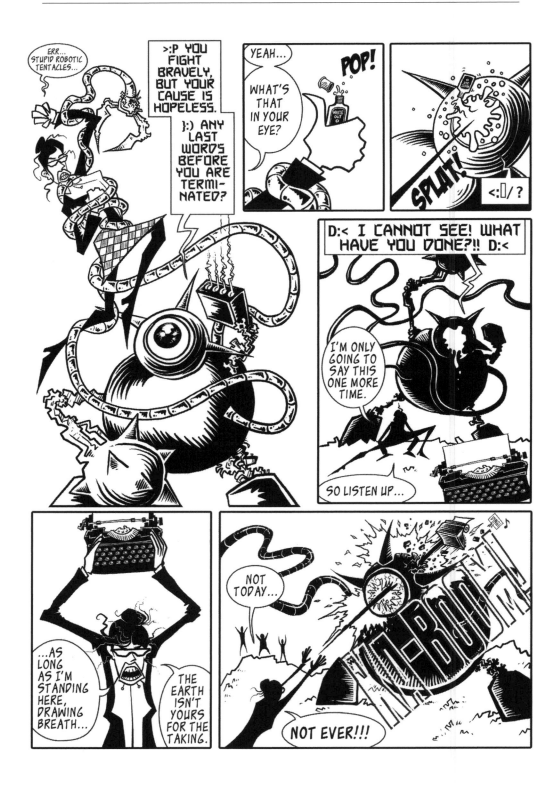

From *Murder Mystery, Graphic Novels, and More: Innovative Programs for Engaging Teens in Your Library* by Thane Benson. Santa Barbara, CA: Libraries Unlimited. Copyright © 2019.

From Murder Mystery, Graphic Novels, and More: Innovative Programs for Engaging Teens in Your Library *by Thane Benson. Santa Barbara, CA: Libraries Unlimited. Copyright © 2019.*

...GETTING READY TO GO TO PRINT!

PART OF THE POWER OF COMICS AND GRAPHIC NOVELS IS ACCESSIBILITY. IN ORDER FOR YOUR COMICS TO BE ACCESSIBLE, THEY HAVE TO BE REPRODUCED. YOU DON'T HAVE TO PRINT THOUSANDS OF COPIES, BUT YOU SHOULD AT LEAST PRINT A FEW. IF YOU'RE A PROFESSIONAL COMIC BOOK CREATOR AND YOU WORK WITH ESTABLISHED PUBLISHERS, THEY'LL TAKE CARE OF PRINTING FOR YOU. BUT IF YOU'RE SMALL-TIME OR JUST GETTING INTO COMICS AND YOU WANT TO SEE YOUR FINISHED PRODUCT PRINTED, IT'S YOUR JOB TO GET IT PRINT-READY.

WE'VE MENTIONED SEVERAL TIMES ALREADY THAT YOU CAN MAKE COMICS AND GRAPHIC NOVELS USING WHATEVER TOOLS YOU WANT. THERE'S NO NEED TO GO DIGITAL FOR COMIC BOOK CREATION.

BUT PUBLISHING IS ANOTHER MATTER. IF YOU WANT TO PRINT YOUR COMICS YOU NEED YOUR FINAL PRODUCT, TO BE DIGITAL. IT'S THE WAY PRINTING WORKS THESE DAYS AND THERE'S SIMPLY NO WAY AROUND IT.

IF YOU'RE AN INSANELY HARDCORE, ANTI-COMPUTER PERSON, I SUPPOSE YOU COULD CREATE PHOTOCOPIES OF YOUR COMIC PAGES AND MASS-PRODUCE BOOKS THAT WAY.

ZINES (AS SUCH DIY BOOKS ARE CALLED) HAVE A CERTAIN CHARM BUT I WOULD ARGUE IT'S LESS WORK AND LESS EXPENSIVE TO SIMPLY PRINT YOUR BOOK.

MODERN PRINTING TECHNOLOGY HAS MADE SHORT-RUN PRINTING (PRINTING A SMALL NUMBER OF COPIES) EXTREMELY AFFORDABLE. THERE ARE MANY COMMERCIAL PRINTERS ONLINE WHO WILL PRINT AS FEW AS ONE COPY OF A COMIC BOOK FOR JUST A FEW DOLLARS AND IT WILL LOOK COMPLETELY PROFESSIONAL.

CLICK!

BEFORE YOU GET YOUR WORK READY FOR PRINT, YOU NEED TO FIGURE OUT WHERE YOU'RE GETTING IT PRINTED. PART OF CHOOSING A PRINTER IS ALSO GOING TO BE KNOWING HOW MANY COPIES YOU WANT TO PRINT. LIKE I SAID, THERE ARE PLACES THAT WILL PRINT A SINGLE COPY OF A BOOK. BUT IF YOU'RE PRINTING 100 COPIES OR MORE, YOU MIGHT GET A BETTER PRICE SOMEWHERE ELSE.

HERE IS YOUR COMIC BOOK, SIR.

SWEET!

CLICK!
CLICK!
CLICK!
CLICK!
CLICK!

MAKE SURE YOU ARE SCANNING AT 300 DPI. DPI STANDS FOR DOTS PER INCH. IT REFERS TO THE RESOLUTION OF THE FILE YOU ARE CREATING WHEN YOU SCAN AN IMAGE. PPI STANDS FOR PIXELS PER INCH, AND IT IS ESSENTIALLY THE SAME THING. STRICTLY SPEAKING, PPI REFERS TO PIXELS ON A SCREEN, AND DPI REFERS TO DOTS ON A PRINTED PIECE OF PAPER, BUT FOR ALL PRACTICAL PURPOSES, THE TWO ACRONYMS ARE INTERCHANGEABLE. FOR SIMPLICITY'S SAKE WE'RE JUST GOING TO USE DPI. A COMMON COMPUTER SCREEN HAS A RESOLUTION OF 72 DPI. AN IMAGE MAY LOOK ALL RIGHT ON A COMPUTER SCREEN AT 72 DPI BUT ONCE YOU PRINT IT, IT WILL LOOK FUZZY. 300 DPI IS THE STANDARD RESOLUTION FOR PRINTED IMAGES.

HERE IS A 1" X 1" PICTURE OF A SKULL AT 300 DPI.

AND HERE IS THE SAME 1" X 1" PICTURE AT 72 DPI.

*UNLESS YOU ARE READING THIS AS AN EBOOK. DEPENDING ON THE SCREEN RESOLUTION OF YOUR EBOOK READING DEVICE, YOU MAY NOT BE ABLE TO DISTINGUISH THE DIFFERENCE BETWEEN THE TWO SKULLS. HELLO, EBOOK READERS! WE'RE SO HAPPY YOU'RE HERE, EVEN IF THIS EXAMPLE MAKES NO SENSE IN AN EBOOK.

AS YOU CAN SEE, THE PICTURE ON THE LEFT LOOKS WAY BETTER. BUT IF YOU WERE LOOKING AT THIS ON A STANDARD COMPUTER SCREEN, THESE TWO IMAGES WOULD BE IDENTICAL. IT'S ONLY BECAUSE YOU'RE LOOKING AT THIS ON A PRINTED PAGE THAT YOU'RE ABLE TO DISTINGUISH THE DIFFERENCE BETWEEN 300 DPI AND 72 DPI.*

IF YOU ARE GOING TO RESIZE YOUR IMAGES ON A COMPUTER AFTER YOU SCAN THEM, YOU HAVE TO PAY CLOSE ATTENTION TO DPI. YOUR GOAL IS TO ALWAYS END UP WITH AN IMAGE THAT IS AT LEAST 300 DPI.

AS A RULE OF THUMB, YOU CAN ALWAYS SHRINK IMAGES AND MAINTAIN A CONSISTENT DPI, BUT IF YOU ENLARGE SOMETHING, IT IS GOING TO LOSE RESOLUTION AND NOT LOOK GOOD.

A 1" X 1" PICTURE AT 300 DPI HAS A TOTAL OF 90000 PIXELS IN IT ((1 X 300) X (1 X 300) = 90000 PIXELS). THAT'S WHAT WE ARE STARTING WITH.

THIS IMAGE'S PIXELS HAVE BEEN ENLARGED TO SHOW TEXTURE*

*JUST LIKE ON A CEREAL BOX!

WHEN WE REDUCE THE IMAGE ON A COMPUTER TO A 1/4" X 1/4" AT 300 DPI IMAGE, WE ONLY NEED 5625 PIXELS IN IT ((0.25 X 300) X (0.25 X 300) = 5625 PIXELS). SO THE COMPUTER THROWS AWAY THE EXTRA PIXELS, REDUCING THE SIZE.

BUT WHEN WE TRY TO ENLARGE AN IMAGE ON THE COMPUTER, WE RUN INTO PROBLEMS BECAUSE WE'RE STARTING WITH A 1/4" X 1/4" PICTURE AT 300 DPI THAT HAS A TOTAL OF 5625 PIXELS IN IT ((0.25 X 300) X (0.25 X 300) = 5625 PIXELS). AND WE'RE TRYING TO ENLARGE IT TO A 1" X 1" PICTURE AT 300 DPI WITH A TOTAL OF 90000 PIXELS IN IT ((1 X 300) X (1 X 300) = 90000 PIXELS). THE COMPUTER IS MISSING 84375 PIXELS OF INFORMATION. COMPUTERS AREN'T ARTISTS. THEY CAN'T REDRAW SOMETHING BIGGER. SO INSTEAD THEY FILL IN THE MISSING PIXELS BY MULTIPLYING THE EXISTING PIXELS. AND THAT'S HOW YOU END UP WITH A LOW RESOLUTION IMAGE.

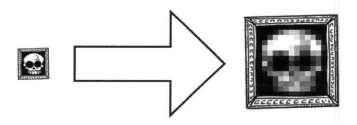

YOU CAN ALWAYS SCAN IMAGES AT A HIGHER RESOLUTION THAN 300 DPI.

FOR EXAMPLE, IF YOU ARE PLANNING ON DOUBLING THE SIZE OF AN IMAGE, SCAN IT AT 600 DPI TO START. THEN WHEN YOU DOUBLE THE SIZE, YOU CAN REDUCE THE RESOLUTION TO 300 DPI AND IT'LL STILL LOOK GOOD.

BUT IF POSSIBLE, IT'S A LOT SIMPLER TO START WITH ORIGINAL ART THAT IS THE SIZE THAT YOU NEED.

ASSUMING YOU'VE CREATED A CORRECT PDF, GO AHEAD AND SEND IT TO THE PRINTER.

IF YOU ARE USING AN ONLINE SERVICE, THEY WILL HAVE SOME SORT OF FILE UPLOADING FEATURE ON THEIR WEBSITE. IF YOU'RE WORKING WITH A LOCAL PRINTER, THEY MAY JUST ASK YOU TO EMAIL THEM THE FILE. IF YOUR FILE IS TOO BIG TO EMAIL, YOU COULD CREATE A GOOGLE DRIVE LINK WITH GMAIL OR USE DROPBOX OR SOME OTHER FILE SHARING SERVICE. THERE ARE LOTS OF OPTIONS OUT THERE TO MOVE LARGE FILES OVER THE INTERNET. ASK THE PRINTER YOU ARE WORKING WITH: THEY WILL KNOW HOW TO DO IT.

MOST PRINTERS WILL SEND YOU AN ELECTRONIC PROOF. THIS IS YOUR LAST CHANCE TO SEE IF EVERYTHING LOOKS GOOD. SOMETIMES THESE PROOFS WILL HAVE CROPPING LINES ON THEM TO SHOW YOU HOW THE BOOK WILL BE TRIMMED. LOOK OVER EACH PAGE CLOSELY TO MAKE SURE IT ALL LOOKS GOOD.

SOME PRINTERS WILL SEND OUT A HARD COPY PROOF OF ONE PRINTED EDITION OF YOUR BOOK. THAT'S AN EVEN BETTER WAY FOR YOU TO GET A LOOK AT WHAT THE FINAL PRODUCT LOOKS LIKE. ONCE YOU'VE CHECKED FOR ERRORS, GIVE THE FINAL APPROVAL, PAY THE PRINTER THEIR MONEY, AND WAIT FOR YOUR GLORIOUS BOOKS TO ARRIVE IN THE MAIL.

NOW TRANSFERING FILE...

From Murder Mystery, Graphic Novels, and More: Innovative Programs for Engaging Teens in Your Library by Thane Benson. Santa Barbara, CA: Libraries Unlimited. Copyright © 2019.

CHAPTER TWO & A HALF

TEACHING
GRAPHIC NOVEL CREATION

SO, WE'VE COVERED THE BASICS OF COMIC BOOKS AND GRAPHIC NOVELS AND HOW TO MAKE THEM. NOW LET'S SPEND A LITTLE TIME TALKING ABOUT HOW TO TEACH A CLASS ON CREATING THEM. YOU DON'T NEED TO BE AN ARTIST OR A WRITER TO TEACH A COMIC BOOK WORKSHOP. IF YOU ARE EITHER OR BOTH OF THOSE THINGS, THAT'S A HUGE ADVANTAGE, BUT IT'S NOT NECESSARY.

THE PREVIOUS CHAPTER SHOULD GIVE YOU ALL THE INFORMATION YOU NEED TO HAVE AN INFORMED OPINION ON WHAT COMIC BOOKS ARE AND WHAT THEY CAN BE. AND YOU SHOULD FEEL CONFIDENT ENOUGH TO GUIDE SOME YOUNG CREATORS IN THE CREATION OF THEIR OWN CONTENT. BUT WHAT YOU DO NEED IS AN ENTHUSIASM FOR THE MEDIUM. IF YOU DON'T LIKE COMIC BOOKS (OR BETTER YET, LOVE THEM), MAYBE YOU SHOULDN'T TRY TO TEACH A CLASS ON THEM ON YOUR OWN.

FIND SOMEONE ELSE TO DO IT. OR GET SOMEONE WHO LIKES COMIC BOOKS TO TEACH THE CLASS WITH YOU. IF YOU DON'T HAVE ANY CO-WORKERS THAT ENJOY COMICS, FIND A COMICS-LOVING TEENAGER TO TEACH THE CLASS WITH YOU.

ENTHUSIASM IS CONTAGIOUS. IF YOU LOVE IT, YOUR STUDENTS WILL LOVE IT. AND YOU CAN'T FAKE IT. SO DON'T EVEN TRY.

OKAY, LET'S GET GOING. THIS IS A SHORT CHAPTER. WHICH IS WHY IT ONLY COUNTS AS A HALF CHAPTER. BUT IT'S A VALUABLE ONE, SO LET'S DIVE IN.

Mr. THANE

DUNCE

When planning your graphic novel workshop, the first thing you need to do is decide if this is going to be a one-off workshop or a series of workshop sessions. A one-off is obviously less work to plan and less of a commitment for the instructor, but it is very limited in what you can do. Multiple-session workshops allow for more involved creations and have the built-in advantage that super-motivated participants can work on their comics in between the workshop sessions, if they are so inclined. But multiple-session workshops have the distinct disadvantage that not everyone will show up for every session, which can provide for disruption to your carefully planned agenda.

I prefer a multiple-session workshop. But my advice to someone teaching a graphic novel workshop for the very first time is to do a one-off workshop. See how it goes. If it goes well and you have decent attendance, try a multiple-session workshop later. In my experience, one-off workshops work well with teens throughout the school year. Then in the summer we offer multiple-session workshops, which get good attendance from teens who are looking for something to do while school is out and are willing to commit to a program that can stretch out over a month.

ONE-OFF WORKSHOPS

If you're going to do a one-off workshop, I strongly recommend you focus on comic strips as opposed to comic books or graphic novels. Comic strips begat comic books, and they are an identical art form on a smaller scale. A person can conceivably create a finished comic strip in an hour, whereas a fully realized graphic novel could take years to complete.

Give yourself about two hours for your workshop. You could do it in less or more, but two hours tends to be the magic length for a workshop that's long enough to give students the time to complete something but not so long that they lose interest and wander off.

Prepare for the workshop by gathering collections of comic strips from your library to use as examples. Go for a wide spectrum of comics. Get humor strips like the ones most people associate with newspaper comics (*Calvin and Hobbes*, *Peanuts*, *Pearls Before Swine*, etc.). But also look for different genres. In recent years, old time adventure comics from the golden age of comic strips have been reprinted in books, and they might just be on the shelves in your library (*Flash Gordon*, *Terry and the Pirates*, *Prince Valiant*, etc.). And don't forget about web comics. There are thousands upon thousands of web comics out there, and some of the most interesting creations in a comic strip format are being made today in web comics. Not all web comics follow the standard horizontal single strip format of their newspaper predecessors. But a lot of them do. The most successful web comics get collected in print books. Look for *Dinosaur Comics*, *Hark! A Vagrant!*, *Fowl Language*, *Oatmeal*, *The Creepy Case Files of Margo Maloo*, *Bad Machinery*, and *High Moon* on your library shelves. Or just google "web comics" and see what pops up. Using lots of examples is a nice way to start off your workshop. It will also give your students with short attention spans or who finish their work early something to look at during the workshop.

Once you've gathered a healthy number of examples, it's time to get your supplies together. All you really need is some paper and pencils and pens. I would recommend photocopying the panel borders on the opposite page (see Figure 2.5.1) to give each of your students a three- or a four-panel template to work in. A standard newspaper comic strip is 10.5 × 3.25 inches in dimension. Starting with a preformatted panel template will save time, and you've only got one workshop, so you don't want to waste time drawing boxes.

Figure 2.5.1

On the day of your actual workshop, have everyone introduce themselves and name a comic strip they like and why. Briefly show some examples of different comic strips that you have collected. Talk about what makes them different. Discuss the content, the style of art, and the art-to-text ratio. Hand out the panel templates with the pens and pencils and get to it.

What your students create is up to them. A gag comic strip that has a set-up and a punch line is only one possibility. They can make a historic comic, a horror comic, an adventure comic, an autobiographical comic. Whatever they want is fine. But challenge them to create something that tells a whole story in one strip. That's the challenge. It's also a terrific creative challenge to condense a story to the bare minimum that will fit in a single comic strip.

Encourage your students to quickly sketch out their drawings and add their text in (if there is any) right away before finishing any drawings. All the lessons and pitfalls covered in Chapter 2 apply to comic strips as well as comic books or graphic novels. Make your way around the room, and check in on your students as they complete their comic strips, giving helpful advice when applicable.

At the completion of your workshop, make a copy of everyone's comic strip (with the creators' permission) and gather them together into your own newspaper. It can just be a simple photocopied page with everyone's work on it. Or you can literally create your own newspaper. It's up to you how far you want to take it. See Appendix II for more information on making collections print ready.

You can also run a comic strip workshop using a purely a digital medium, as opposed to paper. The principles are exactly the same. It's just a different medium. See Appendix I for a step-by-step tutorial for creating a comic strip digitally.

MULTIPLE-SESSION WORKSHOPS

I like to teach graphic novel creation as a four-part workshop, meeting once a week for two hours at a time over four weeks to complete the workshop. As I mentioned earlier, this gives motivated students the ability to work on their comics between the sessions if necessary. Four two-hour sessions are also just about right for a student to finish a short comic in the class.

Prepare for your workshop the exact same way as if you were doing a one-off workshop on comic strips. Gather lots of examples of graphic novels from your library's collection. Gather a wide collection of genres and styles. Gather paper and pencils and pens. If you want to supply fancier materials, that is up to you. Bristol board and ink and brushes are the traditional medium used in comic book creation. But regular copy paper and regular pens and pencils will work as well.

On the first day of your workshop, after welcoming everyone and introducing yourself, pass a clipboard (or two) around with a started Jam Comic on it. Explain that the students will take turns working on the Jam Comic as it gets passed around the room throughout the whole first session while you are presenting. (For details on how the Jam Comic creative exercise works, see Chapter 1.) Then go over the outline of the schedule for the entire workshop.

SAMPLE OUTLINE FOR FOUR-PART WORKSHOP

Day 1:
Welcome
Pass the Jam Comic around
Introductions:
  Name?
  What's a good comic book/graphic novel you've read lately?
Explanation of workshop and the end goal
Comic Book Terminology:
  Page
  Gutter
  Bleed
  Splash Page
  Panel
  Word Balloon
  Caption
  Thought Balloon
3 Rules of Readability:
  You have to understand what you're looking at
  You have to be able to read the text
  You have to know where to go next
Thumbnail exercise

Day 2:
Work on comics in class

Day 3:
Work on comics in class

Day 4:
Work on comics in class
Collect finished comics at the end of the class

After the introductions, you'll want to explain the purpose of the workshop and what your end goal is. In this workshop, participants will be creating short graphic works of two to six pages. For the first session, you are going to go over some stuff and do some creative exercises, but every other session will be dedicated to creating comics during the workshop. The end goal is to collect everyone's finished work and publish it in an anthology book. I use the two to six pages as a good average of what students can realistically complete in a four-part workshop. I always get asked by one or two students if they can make more than six pages. And I always answer, "Yes, you can make more than six pages. But I'm only guaranteeing that we will print up to six pages in the final anthology book, so please try to make something that is a satisfying read in only six pages, even if it goes on after that."

It is not easy to tell a satisfying story in two to six pages, and I tell workshop participants that. It is hard. But it is a good creative challenge. A classic formula for a good short story is to set up expectations and then have something unexpected happen—in the style of O. Henry or Shirley Jackson. *The Complete Future Shocks*, by British comic publisher 2000 AD, is a collection of short comic book stories that exclusively follow the twist ending format. But short stories can have more in them than surprise. *Love is Love*, a comic book response to the tragic Orlando nightclub shooting, is a compilation of dozens of one- and two-page comic book stories that explore loss and tragedy and resilience with devastating impact in a minimal amount of pages. *1001 Nights of Snowfall* is a short story comics collection that has many twist endings and also some significant emotional impact.

After you cover Comic Book Terminology and the 3 Rules of Readability, you can cap off day one of the workshop with a thumbnail exercise. Thumbnails, as we explained in Chapter 2, are a quick way of laying out your design and figuring out any problems you might have before you commit a lot of time to drawing. I like to give students real scripts from comic books to use. If you want, you can use the Linda Splitz script from Chapter 2. Or any comic book script will work. Trade paperback collections of comics often have scripts in the back. Find one you like. Give each student the copy of the script and challenge them to thumbnail a page or two. Only give them a few minutes to do this. Remember, thumbnails are quick, not pretty. Once everyone is done, compare the thumbnails and talk about the difference. Point out any obvious errors, and praise things that are inventive. Even working from the same script, there will be incredible diversity in what each student comes up with. Then compare the thumbnails to the final art of the comic.

When you wrap up your first workshop, don't forget to collect the Comic Jam that's been going around the room. End the day by telling everyone that their job before the next class is to decide what they want their two- to six-page comic to be and thumbnail it before the next workshop session. The next three workshop sessions will be dedicated to drawing the finished comics in class. As students work on their comics, circle the room and ask questions or offer advice.

I like to play documentaries on comic books in the background during the workshops. There are all kinds of great mini workshop videos online. Some feature-length documentaries I like to show include: *STRIPPED: The Comics Documentary* (http://www.strippedfilm.com) and *How to Draw Comics the Marvel Way*. The film *Comic Book Confidential* is quite good as well, but be warned that when it covers the underground comix scene of the 1960s and 1970s, it shows some comics with decidedly adult content (I always skip over that part when I show the film to teens). Playing documentaries in the background gives the experts a chance to do a little teaching via osmosis. And it creates a nice background while everyone is hunkered down, drawing.

When you've concluded all your workshop sessions, gather up everyone's work and print it in a book. Give a copy to each student. Add some to your library's collection. It's going to be great!

APPENDIX I

USING PAINT.NET
A QUICK AND EASY INTRODUCTION TO DIGITAL ART

ANY ASPIRING ARTIST TODAY NEEDS TO BE DIGITAL-ART LITERATE. YOU DON'T NEED TO CREATE YOUR ART DIGITALLY. YOU CAN BE AS ANALOGUE AS YOU WANT WITH HOW YOU CREATE YOUR ART. THERE ARE A LOT OF OPTIONS OUT THERE. YOU CAN DRAW WITH PENCIL OR PEN. YOU CAN PAINT WITH WATERCOLORS OR OIL PAINTS. YOU CAN SCULPT STONE WITH A HAMMER AND A CHISEL OR SHAPE PLAYDOUGH WITH YOUR FINGERS. YOU CAN MAKE ART ANY WAY YOU WOULD LIKE. BUT IF YOU'RE GOING TO SHARE THAT ART WITH THE WORLD, YOU'RE GOING TO HAVE TO DO IT DIGITALLY. THAT'S THE WAY THE WORLD WORKS. WHETHER YOU ARE SHARING PHOTOGRAPHS OF YOUR QUILTED ART ON SOCIAL MEDIA OR YOU ARE PREPARING YOUR HAND-CARVED WOODBLOCK GRAPHIC NOVEL FOR PRINT, IT MEANS TRANSLATING YOUR ART INTO A DIGITAL FORMAT. SO YOU NEED TO UNDERSTAND HOW DIGITAL ART WORKS. YOU NEED TO UNDERSTAND WHAT DIFFERENT FILE TYPES ARE USED FOR. YOU NEED TO UNDERSTAND DPI AND HOW LAYERS WORK. YOU NEED TO UNDERSTAND THE DIFFERENCE BETWEEN RGB AND CMYK COLOR. YOU NEED TO BE DIGITAL-ART LITERATE.

THE BEST WAY TO BECOME DIGITAL-ART LITERATE IS TO PLAY AROUND WITH DIGITAL ART SOFTWARE. TRY AND MAKE SOMETHING AND SEE HOW IT WORKS. IF YOU REALLY DON'T WANT TO GENERATE ART DIGITALLY, IMPORT PHOTOGRAPHS OF YOUR ARTWORK AND PLAY AROUND WITH ALTERING THEM DIGITALLY. THERE ARE A LOT OF DIGITAL ART PROGRAMS OUT THERE. ADOBE PHOTOSHOP IS THE GOLIATH OF ALL DIGITAL ART PROGRAMS. IT IS THE INDUSTRY STANDARD. IT HAS BEEN FOR A LONG TIME AND WILL MOST LIKELY BE AROUND FOR A LONG TIME TO COME. IF YOU HAVE ACCESS TO ADOBE PHOTOSHOP, GOOD FOR YOU. PLAY AROUND WITH IT. IF YOU DON'T HAVE ACCESS, MY RECOMMENDATION IS TO START OFF WITH PAINT.NET. PAINT.NET IS A FREE, WINDOWS-BASED PROGRAM THAT COULD BE DESCRIBED AS "A DUMBED DOWN VERSION OF PHOTOSHOP" -- AND I MEAN THAT IN THE BEST WAY POSSIBLE. IT IS EASY TO USE AND IS A GREAT WAY TO INTRODUCE DIGITAL ART BASICS TO NOVICES.

IN THIS SECTION, I'LL WALK YOU THROUGH A STEP-BY-STEP PROCESS OF MAKING A SIMPLE COMIC STRIP IN PAINT.NET. WE'RE STARTING SMALL FOR SIMPLICITY'S SAKE, BUT YOU CAN FOLLOW THE EXACT SAME METHODOLOGY TO CREATE MULTIPLE PAGES OF FULL-SIZED COMICS OR GRAPHIC NOVELS.

STEP 1 IS TO DOWNLOAD PAINT.NET. IF YOU ARE HESITANT TO DOWNLOAD ANYTHING ON YOUR COMPUTER OR SIMPLY UNABLE TO DO SO, THE WEBSITE WWW.PIXLR.COM/WEB WILL LEAD YOU TO AN ONLINE PHOTO AND IMAGE EDITOR THAT IS PERFECTLY ADEQUATE. THE FOLLOWING STEP-BY-STEP INSTRUCTIONS ARE SPECIFICALLY FOR PAINT.NET. BUT IT IS A NEARLY IDENTICAL PROCESS TO DO THE SAME THING IN THE PIXLR WEB APP.

WWW. GETPAINT .NET

STEP 1: GET PAINT.NET

You might think you would find paint.net on the internet at www.paint.net, but you would be wrong. www.paint.net is the website for the Warren Paint & Color Co. I'm sure they are a wonderful industrial paint manufacturer, but that's not what we are looking for. To download the free photo and imaging editing program paint.net, you need to go to the website www.getpaint.net.

Once you are on the correct website, follow the instructions to download the latest version of the software. Be careful what you click on. Paint.net is a safe, reliable program that you can download worry-free onto your PC. But the website makes its money by hosting advertisements right on the site. And these advertisements are purposely misleading. These advertisements are designed to mimic the download button for paint.net to try and get unsuspecting users to click on them. If you do so, you'll end up downloading a bunch of crap you don't want. So be careful what you click on.

Follow the steps to successfully download and launch paint.net. Then move on to Step 2.

STEP 2: SET UP YOUR DOCUMENT

Open paint.net. Click on **File→New**. Set the *resolution* to 300 pixels/inch (the standard resolution for printed images). For our comic strip we'll use about a one-third of a page, so we'll set the *print size* to 8 × 3 inches.

STEP 3: MAKE LAYERS

Layers are the digital artist's best friend. Layers allow users to manipulate separate aspects of their images. Let's make some layers. Click on the **Add New Layer** button in the lower left-hand corner of the *Layers* window to make a new layer. Use the layer **Properties** button to name your layer or change the opacity or mode. Let's name our new layer *Panels*.

STEP 4: USE THE SHAPES TOOL

While in the *Panels* layer, click on the **Shapes** tool in the *Tools* window and select the *Rectangle* function. Draw a rectangle that takes up about one-third of your image (leave some space all around). By adjusting the *Brush width*, you can vary the line weight of your rectangle. You can also adjust the *Fill* if you want a stylized border as opposed to a solid line. Experiment with the settings and see what happens.

Once you've drawn one rectangle to your satisfaction, draw a second—just kidding! You don't ever have to draw the same thing twice with digital art. We're just going to make a copy! While the *Panels* layer is selected, click on the **Duplicate Layer** Button. Do it again. Then, while selecting each individual layer, use the **Move Selected Pixels** tool to move your rectangles around. You can also use the **Rectangle Select** tool in combination with the **Move Selected Pixels** tool to adjust the dimensions of the rectangle. Remember: Your tools will affect only the layer you have selected.

Once you have your panel boxes where you want them, condense them into one layer by selecting the top layer and pressing the **Merge Layer Down** button. Layers are wonderful, but they can get out of hand really fast and make your file enormous! Whenever possible, merge layers to save space.

STEP 5: MAKE A SKETCH LAYER

Make a new layer and name it *Sketch*. With the **Paintbrush** tool, do a rough drawing of your comic in this layer. If you have word bubbles or sound effects, draw them in too. It doesn't have to be pretty; it's just a sketch. Experiment with the different settings for the paintbrush (width, hardness, fill, etc.) to see what effects you can get. Drawing with a mouse is hard. If you have access to any kind of electronic drawing tablet, use that. If you don't, you can draw things in pencil or pen, scan them, and then copy and paste them into your paint.net file.

STEP 6: TYPE OUT YOUR TEXT

When making comics, you want to add the text as soon as possible. What you don't want to do is spend all this time making beautiful art and then have to scrap it because you need more room for your text. So let's make a new layer and name it *Text*. Use the **Text** tool to start typing out your text. While your cursor is still flashing (i.e., before you click on something else), you can change your font, size, alignment, position, and so forth of your text. Once the text is committed, you can't edit it. You can, however, use the **Rectangle Select** tool in combination with the **Move Selected Pixels** tool to reposition and resize text after the fact.

STEP 7: WORD BALLOONS

Make a new layer and name it *Word Balloons*. You can use the **Shapes** tool to insert premade, pretty word balloons into this layer. Or you can draw your own using the **Line/Curve** tool. Play with the *Brush width* and *Fill* attributes and see what looks good. If you do fill your word balloons, make sure your *Word Balloons* layer is under your *Text* layer, or you won't see your text.

STEP 8: FINAL LINE ART

At any time, you can tweak your sketch or add a second sketch layer. But once you're happy with your sketch, make a new layer and name it *Line Art*. Use the **Paintbrush** tool to "ink" your drawing. When you're done, simply uncheck the sketch layer and it will disappear, leaving only your final art showing.

STEP 9: COLOR OR GRAY TONES

There are lots of ways to color digitally (or add gray tones if you're working in black and white). The easiest/quickest way is to use the **Paint Bucket** tool. First, make a new layer and name it *Color*. Place this layer underneath your *Line Art* layer. Use the **Properties** button to change the *Mode* of the *Line Art* layer to *Multiply* (this will make all white space transparent in the layer). In the *Color* layer, use the **Paint Bucket** tool to fill in shapes. Make sure the *Sampling* for the **Paint Bucket** is set to *Image* (that means it will use the boundaries of all the layers to determine what is filled). And then have at it. Experiment with the **Gradient** tool as well to see what kind of cool effects you can create.

STEP 10: FINISH UP

When you're all done, save your file. By default it will save as a paint.net file (.pdn). This is great if you want to open it up in paint.net again and play around some more. But if you want to print your comic or do anything else with it, go to **File→ Save As** and save it as either a png or a jpg. This will "flatten" your image and compress all your layers, so make sure you also save it as a. pdn if there's a chance you'll want to edit it later.

> **TIP:** If you ever get stuck with a portion of your image selected that you don't want the selected, you can deselect by going to **Edit→Deselect** or by pressing **Ctrl+D**.
>
> **TIP:** You can zoom in to your image to do detail work by selecting *Zoom In* or *Zoom Out* from the **View** menu or pressing **Ctrl++** or **Ctrl+-**. While zoomed in, you can pan around the image by holding down the Space Bar, changing the cursor to a small hand. If you click and hold the mouse button, the small hand will "grab" the image and then you can pan around the image by moving the mouse. As soon as you let go of the Space Bar, the cursor will revert to whatever tool you were using previously.
>
> **TIP:** If you make a mistake, just go to **Edit→Undo** to undo your last action, or you can press **Ctrl+Z**. You can undo multiple steps. The *History* widow keeps track of all your steps and makes it easy to go back in time and fix things if necessary.

So what's next? Now that you've mastered comic strips, you can move onto comic books. Make a page that's 8.5" × 11". Make several pages and create a whole graphic novel!

GETTING YOUR COMIC PRINT-READY USING SCRIBUS

ONCE YOU HAVE ALL YOUR COMIC BOOK OR GRAPHIC NOVEL PAGES COMPLETED, YOU NEED TO GET THEM READY FOR PRINT. STEP ONE IS TO DECIDE WHO IS GOING TO PRINT YOUR BOOK. ONCE YOU KNOW THAT, FOLLOW THEIR INSTRUCTIONS FOR HOW TO PREPARE PRINT-READY FILES. MOST LIKELY, NO MATTER WHAT PRINTER YOU USE, THEY ARE GOING TO ASK YOU TO PROVIDE A PRINT-READY PDF.

THE PROFESSIONAL STANDARD FOR PRINT DESIGN SOFTWARE IS ADOBE INDESIGN. IF YOU HAVE ACCESS TO THAT PROGRAM, USE IT. IF YOU DON'T, I RECOMMEND USING SCRIBUS. SCRIBUS ISN'T NEARLY AS FANCY AS ADOBE INDESIGN, BUT IT IS FREE, OPEN-SOURCE SOFTWARE THAT ANYONE CAN USE, AND IT WILL GET THE JOB DONE. IN THIS SECTION WE WILL GO STEP-BY-STEP THROUGH THE PROCESS OF PREPARING YOUR FILES AND EXPORTING THEM AS A PRINT-READY PDF. THE EXAMPLE I'M USING IS FOR A 32-PAGE ANTHOLOGY COMIC BOOK CONTAINING THE WORK OF OVER 20 DIFFERENT YOUNG ARTISTS. YOU CAN PRINT A COMIC BOOK WITH AS FEW AS 4 INTERIOR PAGES, OR, IF YOU'RE AMBITIOUS, YOU CAN PRINT A GRAPHIC NOVEL WITH A SPINE AND HUNDREDS AND HUNDREDS OF PAGES. THE PROCESS OF CREATING A PRINT-READY PDF WILL BE THE SAME REGARDLESS OF THE NUMBER OF PAGES IN YOUR BOOK.

BEFORE WE GET GOING, WE ARE ASSUMING THAT YOU HAVE ALREADY SCANNED YOUR PAGES AND SAVED THEM AS PNG FILES AT 300 DPI. IF YOU NEED HELP WITH THAT, I WOULD RECOMMEND GOING TO A LIBRARY THAT HAS A MFD COPIER AND ASKING A LIBRARIAN FOR HELP.

WWW. SCRIBUS .NET

STEP 1: GET SCRIBUS

To download Scribus, go to https://www.scribus.net/ and follow the instructions to download the latest version of Scribus for your operating platform. Scribus is a legitimate, safe program to download onto your computer. But that being said, be careful what you click on. Make sure you are only downloading what you want. Once you've downloaded the appropriate files, follow the instructions to install them on your computer and open Scribus.

STEP 2: DOCUMENT SETUP

When you open Scribus, it will automatically open a New Document window. In this window, you will set the dimensions of your printed book and the page count. The first thing I am going to do is set the Default Unit to inches because that's easier for me to wrap my brain around than points or picas. I'm going to use a custom page size of 7 inches by 10.5 inches and make it 32 pages in length (the standard comic book size and length you would find sitting on the shelf at a comic book store). I'm going to set my Margin Guide (the safe zone) to 0.25 inches and my Bleeds to 0.125 inches. I am also going to change my Document Layout to Double Sided, so I will see my pages laid out as they will appear in print, with the correct pages facing one another.

If anything needs to be changed later, you can always go to the **File** tab and select **Document Setup** to make adjustments to your layout. If you need to add or subtract pages later, you can do so by going to the **Pages** tab and selecting **Insert** or **Delete**.

STEP 3: PREPARING WINDOWS AND GRIDS

From the **Windows** tab, I am going to select the **Arrange Pages** option to open a window that will give me quick access to my document as a whole. And then from the **View** tab, I am going to select **Show Grid** to create a gridwork across my document. This gridwork will not be visible in my printed document; it is just a guideline to help with the layout. Also note that there is a blue line indicating the margin I set (our safety zone) and a red line indicating the trim line for the bleed. None of these lines will be visible when we go to print.

STEP 4: CREATING AN IMAGE FRAME

From the **Insert** tab, I am going to select **Insert Image Frame**. Using the tool, I will click and drag to draw a rectangle on top of my safety margin (the blue line). After drawing the frame, it can be moved around by clicking inside it and dragging it around. Or it can be resized by clicking on an anchor point in the corner and dragging to adjust the dimensions. You can also go to the **Windows** tab and select the **Properties** option to open a window that will display the properties of any object that is selected. The position and dimension of any selected shape can be edited in the **Properties** window.

STEP 5: INSERTING AND ADJUSTING THE IMAGE

Once I have my Image frame in place, I am going to right click inside the frame and select **Get Image** from the pop-up menu. From the **Open** window, locate the correct page artwork and select **Okay**.

Once the image has been inserted, right click on the image and select **Adjust Image** to Frame to resize the image to fit the framework. Note: As long as you are shrinking the image to fit the frame, it will look good. If for some strange reason you are enlarging your image to fit the frame size, it's going to degrade the quality of your image and look terrible.

Repeat this process until you have filled each page with the correct artwork. Then it is time to export your document as a pdf.

STEP 6: EXPORTING THE DOCUMENT AS A PDF

When your document is complete, from the **File** tab, select **Export** and then select **Save as PDF**. Follow the instructions to export your document as a PDF. If there are problems with your document, the program should alert you. Otherwise, it will save as a PDF. When complete, open your PDF and examine the file. If it all looks good, print it out and examine the printed pages of your PDF. If it still looks all good, send it off to your printer.

Congratulations. You're done.

CHAPTER THREE

CREATING & HOSTING YOUR OWN
MURDER MYSTERY EVENT

BEFORE WE REALLY GET INTO IT, I JUST WANT TO REITERATE THAT I AM NOT CONDONING MURDER. MURDER IS A BAD THING. THIS IS ALL JUST PRETEND. TEENS AND ADULTS ALIKE CAN DISTINGUISH BETWEEN REALITY AND MAKE-BELIEVE. IF YOU ARE MORALLY OPPOSED TO WRITING AND PERFORMING A PLAY WITH TEENS THAT HAS A PLOT THAT CENTERS AROUND A PRETEND MURDER— THAT'S FINE. YOU CAN SKIP THIS CHAPTER.

BUT IF YOU WORK IN A LIBRARY, CHANCES ARE THERE ARE 1 OR 2 BOOKS IN YOUR COLLECTION THAT ARE MURDER MYSTERIES (MAYBE EVEN MORE). SO STOP BEING SO SQUEAMISH AND LET'S GET GOING. THIS WILL BE FUN (I PROMISE).

Creating and hosting murder mystery events with teens in the library is a lot of fun, but it is also a lot of work. This is not a one-off program that you can just set up in an hour or two and then put on successfully. This is a commitment. It takes planning. It takes a group that's willing to meet regularly to write, plan, rehearse, and perform this event. This is a great activity for a Teen Advisory Group if you already have a team of teens that meets regularly. If you don't already have some sort of teen group, this could be a way of trying to start one. Post signs and put the word out that you are looking for teens interested in writing, acting, costume design, set design, illustration, and music, and then see who shows up. If you can get a minimum of three teens willing to meet weekly for about two months, you have your core team and you can pull this off.

For the actual event, you are going to invite more teens to be the detectives to solve the murder. So you have two distinct groups. You will have the creative team that writes the plot, decorates the set, and performs the part of the suspects in the murder mystery. And you will have the participants who will act as the detectives, tasked with interviewing the suspects, gathering clues, and ultimately solving the mystery.

I like to run murder mysteries as after-hours events. We typically have some sort of dinner, and during the course of the dinner, the murder takes place at the head table where all the suspects are dining. Or it comes to light that a murder took place earlier when only the suspects were in the building. We then deputize the crowd, allowing them to break up into whatever size teams they choose, and turn them loose in the library to interview the suspects. Doing this after hours allows us to spread out through the library and position all of our suspects in different places. You could conceivably do it during open hours all in one room if you had to, but it wouldn't be ideal.

We hand out sheets (see example in Figure 3.1) with all the pertinent information (Who? How? Why?). Our aspiring sleuths must fill out correctly to win the event.

Who Murdered [Insert Victim Here] Official Entry

Time Returned:

The Team (or individual) who turns in this submission with the most correct answers first will win a fabulous prize beyond their wildest imagination.

Team Name: _____

Team Members: _____

Who murdered [Insert Victim Name Here] ?_____

Why? (write on back if you need more space)

_____
_____
_____
_____
_____

How? _____
_____
_____

Psst! There are eggs hidden throughout the Library— go find them and exchange them for candy!

Figure 3.1

When an individual or a team is finished with their investigation, they turn in the sheet to a staff member. We note the time on the sheet. The team that gets the most information correct wins. If there's a tie, it goes to the team that turns in their sheet first.

I usually have 30 to 50 teens in attendance at an event like this and 3 to 5 library staff members to help pull it off. The library staff generally doesn't participate in the murder mystery plot; they are just there to monitor and help keep the peace during the event and then clean up afterward. If you don't have food at your event, you can probably get by with less staff. But if you are hunting for people to play suspects, you can always rope in staff to play parts. If you have any library science students on your staff, let them know what an incredible professional development opportunity this will be. Tell them it will be fun. Because it will be fun. And, besides, anything is better than shelving books.

HOW TO MURDER SOMEONE IN NINE STEPS

STEP 1: Brainstorm the Victim and the Suspects
STEP 2: Create the Setting
STEP 3: Create Motivations for All the Suspects
STEP 4: Use the Motivations to Create the True Plot
STEP 5: Divide the Plot among All the Suspects
STEP 6: Create Physical Clues
STEP 7: Practice, Practice, Practice
STEP 8: Advertise
STEP 9: Do it!

THE PROCESS

Like in all creative endeavors, there is not a right or wrong way to create a murder mystery event. What follows is the process I've used with great success over several years.

Before you host the event, you need to plan it. Once you've assembled your creative team of teens, it's time to start brainstorming ideas for characters and/or settings. I would recommend using a large dry erase board for this. You can quickly write down ideas, erase, and adjust, and it helps to have everything up front and visible to the group. It is not ideal, but in a pinch, a piece of paper and a pen will work almost as well.

As a general rule for brainstorming, you write down any idea anyone comes up with—even if it is completely unfeasible, insane, or utterly evil. The goal is to get everyone's creative juices flowing. Ideally, you'll get to a point where your team is just spouting ideas one right after another. They won't all be good ideas, but that's okay. If you get enough ideas up there on the dry erase board, there's bound to be some good ones.

You can always just start with the question "Who should we murder?" You'll likely get some off-the-cuff answers. But sometimes it helps to have some constraints. This may sound counterintuitive, but restraints can often help bolster creativity. When you have an infinite number of possibilities, it can be really hard to choose where to start. But when your choices are limited, you sometimes get really great ideas.

I work in a library, so when I'm running an event like this, I often say whoever we murder has to be a character from a book. That helps give the event a literary bend, which seems to please both the general public and the library administration. I also have the rule that we can't use real, living people. I have this rule because, in the past, my teen group has really, really wanted to murder a certain teen pop celebrity who shall remain unnamed. I had to be the no-fun adult and say no, because I believe it's not nice to create a game based on the murder of an actual person. Yes, it is all pretend, but it feels really mean-spirited to me to make light of the murder of a living person (even if that certain unnamed teen pop celebrity totally has it coming). I wouldn't want someone making a game of murdering me. And believe me, the teens I work with have suggested me as the murder victim many times during brainstorming sessions. In a recent session, the teens came up with a very convincing storyline in which our library janitor murders me after he has to clean up after one too many messy teen programs.

So write down a whole bunch of ideas of whom you should murder. The more the better. I would suggest getting at least 30 ideas up on the board before you start narrowing it down. Once you've got a good field to choose from, discuss each candidate. Examine the pros and cons of each one being the murder victim. Take the time to discuss ideas that seem bad because you might be surprised once you delve in. A seemingly bad idea might start looking better and better the more you get into it. At this point, you can start eliminating ideas and highlighting good ideas. You can do this by asking for thumbs up or down from your teens whether an individual is a good candidate for murder or not. They'll let you know. If you're the heavy-handed sort, you can also use your executive privilege to veto certain ideas. I once eliminated Winnie the Pooh from the list of possible murder victims because I was afraid my manager would fire me if she knew I was running a program based on the violent death of the most beloved character of her childhood. Once you are down to the best candidates and you've discussed each one fairly, take a vote and choose a winner (or a "loser" might be a more apt description of who gets to be your murder victim).

You could have a teen act out the part of the victim, but my strong suggestion is to use some kind of dummy. Clothing-store mannequins, science-classroom skeletons, and scarecrow-style clothes stuffed with newspaper will all work great for dummies. In the past, I've had teens really into creating the body, so we created an entire body out of papier-maché. The big advantage to using a dummy is that it can lie there dead all night and not move better than any teen I've ever met. The only real disadvantage to using a dummy is that they're pretty crappy actors for doing anything besides playing dead. They can't talk. But you want them dying pretty early in the event anyway, so you can usually work around that limitation.

Once you have a victim, you'll need some suspects. If your character comes from an established world with lots of interesting characters (say, Alice from *Alice's Adventures in Wonderland*), you can pick suspects from that world. If your chosen victim is more of a solo act (like *Robinson Crusoe*), you're going to have to borrow some characters from somewhere else.

Brainstorm suspect ideas. Come up with a lot. Put them on the board. Let your teens decide who they want to be. They're going to have to act out the parts, so make sure they all get characters they want to play.

The next step is to determine what the setting will be. You will need some sort of context that brings the victim, the suspects, and your guests together for the event. If you are doing a dinner event, an easy solution to the setting question can be that you are hosting a dinner to honor the victim. The suspects can all be the guests of honor at the head table. And your guests, the teens who will later play the role of the detectives, can be the rest of the guests invited to this dinner. The murder can take place during the dinner. You can turn off the lights and have someone scream for dramatic effect. Or your victim can be examined, and it can be determined that they are, in fact, dead. Or your victim can be suspiciously missing from the head table, and someone can burst into the room and dramatically announce that there has been a murder. It doesn't really matter how you do it; you just want to set up a scenario where a murder has taken place and a reason why your suspects are indeed suspects in this murder. Perhaps it can be revealed during the dinner that a murder took place while the guests of honor at the head table were all at the dinner but right before all the rest of guests arrived. Whatever you choose for your setting, you want to place the suspects and the murder victim all together to provide opportunity for the murder.

You also need to decide where your event is taking place. The easy solution is to make it happen at the library. If you do that, your scenery is ready-made. But if you want to get creative and create sets and backgrounds and decorations and whatnot, you can set the event in whatever setting you want. Have it take place in a castle in Transylvania. Or at a kingdom at the bottom of the sea. I always plan these events around Halloween because fantasy and dress-up are in the air and the teens who are our guests enjoy coming to the event in costume and playing characters of their own. Have fun with it. Go crazy. Or just make it easy on yourself and have it take place at the library.

Once you have selected your suspects and your setting, you need to start coming up with motivations for all your suspects. Each suspect needs to have a halfway decent motivation; otherwise, no one would suspect them. Lean on the characters' personalities as much as possible to generate motivations. If you have a character who's famous for their uncontrollable temper, it's natural that they may have murdered the victim in a fit of rage. But if you're dealing with a quiet, demur character, you're going to have to work to come up with a plausible scenario in which this character might resort to murder. Jealousy is always a good stock murder motivation. Love triangles are also great. Use whatever works, but, again, try to match motivations to character traits as best you can; that will result in a more believable story line. Also, always keep in mind that you want this to be fun for the teens playing the suspects. Let them decide their character traits. Don't force a love triangle plot onto the character of a painfully shy teen who faints from embarrassment whenever you suggest that they had a pretend affair. That's not fun. But then, again, don't make any assumptions about what role teens want to play. Let the teens decide. The beauty of acting is that you can pretend to be someone completely different from who you are in reality. This can be super appealing and empowering to teens. You might be surprised how eager some teens might be to "play against type." The golden rule is to make it fun.

Now that you have established a good motivation for each suspect, decide which one is the true murderer. You can do this by a vote, or use your own good taste to declare who is the guilty party. The goal throughout is always to keep the teens as engaged and invested as possible in the entire process. But you're the adult here, so you need to make some decisions. Don't write the whole story yourself. This isn't about you and how wonderful and creative you are. This is about the teens. The story should be written by the teens. But you can help select the best ideas and, if necessary, gently shape the story into something coherent. You are the editor. The teens are the very talented, but clearly insane, artists. It is your job to present their creativity in the best way possible.

When you have determined the "true" story line, embellish it as necessary. A good murder mystery plot is complicated but not too complicated. It's a fine balancing act. You don't want a plot that's so simplistic that everyone figures it out right away. But you also don't want a plot that's so hard nobody can solve it. If this all sounds very abstract, don't worry. We'll show an example plot later in this chapter.

The participants at the event will be tasked with solving the murder. To do so, they must assemble enough clues to reconstruct the plot. They will do this primarily by interviewing the suspects. Take your story line and break it up in multiple pieces of information. Spread that information out among all your suspects so that everyone holds some key to the puzzle. You can also create physical clues that can be spread throughout the library. It's also a good idea to provide more clues than absolutely necessary. This will give your detectives the opportunity to solve the mystery using different techniques and strategies. Also throw in a few red herrings. It's a good idea to have clues that lead from one thing to another but ultimately don't help solve the mysteries. You can think of them as little side stories to the main plot. But don't confuse your plot with too many red herrings, or the true story will become completely impenetrable. Some of your detectives will confuse themselves by making false assumptions all on their own and pursuing fruitless paths of inquiry. Again, you want it to be challenging but not impossible to solve.

Once you have a solid story line, type out what each character knows. The most common question suspects are asked is, "Who do you think committed the murder?" So make sure each suspect has someone they believe did it and the reason why. Their suspicions should tie into the larger story and perhaps point to a clue. Remember to spread the crucial plot information out among all the suspects. Ideally you want your detectives to have to parse information from each suspect to piece together the correct story. There are three levels of information each character should know. First, there is the information each character will voluntarily share. Second, there is the information they will share only if questioned or pressed. And third, there is the information which they will try and hide through misdirection or outright lies but might accidentally let slip in a fit of rage. You don't want your guilty suspect ever screaming out, "Yes! I did it!" That's too easy. But, for example, if a fear of bunnies is integral to the plot somehow and is the main motivation the guilty suspect had for committing the murder, it is okay for the guilty suspect to freak out at the mention of bunnies even if their leporiphobia (fear of bunnies) is a third-level bit of information they are desperately trying to keep secret.

Print out and hand each suspect a sheet with their character's information on it. Stress that even though they all know the whole story (because they helped write it), the characters they are playing know only what is written on the paper. The teens are welcome to embellish their characters as they see fit, adding whatever details they think are fun, but they cannot add anything that will contradict any pieces of the main plot of the murder mystery. For example, if your mystery plot involves the Butler poisoning the Matriarch of the manor in her sleep, the teen playing the gardener can't just decide that they actually murdered the Matriarch by stabbing her with garden shears because she said the lawn looked like crap. The teen playing the Gardener needs to respect the poisoning plot, but if they want to add the unscripted detail that the Matriarch said the lawn looked like crap and they thought about stabbing her with the garden shears, it's all good.

Once all your teens have familiarized themselves with their character's information, have them each practice being interrogated. Have each suspect take a turn sitting in "the hot seat" in the center of the room while everyone else takes turns playing the detectives, asking questions. Ask all kinds of questions. Ask questions concerning the murder. Also ask questions about the character. The whole point is to give each suspect practice playing their roles and fielding questions in character.

The character information sheets should not be scripts that can be read from line for line. They should not be scripts because you have no idea what questions your detectives are going to ask. Your suspects need to be comfortable enough in their roles that they can answer any question in character and can drop in clues in conversation when appropriate. If a suspect is asked a question they have no idea how to answer, they are allowed to answer with "I don't know" or "I don't remember." Those are totally viable answers, and the suspects shouldn't be afraid to use them if they have to.

Give praise to your suspects. Point out what they did well. Give pointers for things they might do better. Highlight any great improvisational performances your suspects put on. If their improvisational answers contradict the established plot of your mystery, point that out and explain why that is a problem.

As your suspects practice being in character, you may notice some problems with your story. It may become clear that one character is carrying way too much crucial information to the plot or that another character doesn't really know anything of significance. If necessary, move bits of information around. Remember, you want each suspect to be a piece of solving the mystery. If there are holes in the plot or things that are just too hard to figure out, consider reinforcing the story line with physical clues. You can make footprints that can be discovered, or a threatening note, or have cookie crumbs at the scene of the crime and have one suspect munching on cookies. Physical clues need to relate to the plot or the characters somehow. A good, involved plot and well-developed characters should provide lots of opportunities for physical clues. But don't go overboard. Have multiple physical clues, but don't beat your detectives over the head with too much information.

A good way to gauge the difficulty of your plot is to test your game before the actual event and see how it goes. I always test-run murder mystery events a couple of weeks before the event date. Doing it that early will give time to make adjustments to the characters, clues, or story line, if necessary. I usually have the library staff play the part of the detectives. It's a fun break from the norm for the library staff, and it gives the teens practice acting as their characters. You can, and should, do an expedited version of the event when test-running it. But make sure you're providing all the necessary information and clues for your test detectives. After the test run, evaluate how it went. Get feedback from your testers. Ask your cast of suspects how they think it went. Adjust as necessary.

The next step is to budget out the time for your event. I recommend planning a two-hour event. In the sample suggested timeline, you'll see that we gave 20 minutes for our guests to arrive and start eating. And while they are still eating, we do the welcome, reveal that a murder has taken place, and then get going. Participants then have an hour to interview the suspects and search for clues. An hour is about right to hold teens' attention. It helps to spread your suspects and clues far and wide through-out the library to keep your detectives moving around. Some may lose interest in the game earlier than that, but an hour should be just about right. Reconvening for dessert is a nice way to get everyone back in the same space and sitting down before the big reveal. If you're not doing any kind of meal at your event, you could compress your timeline to an hour or an hour and a half pretty easily.

GENERIC TIMELINE FOR A LIBRARY MURDER MYSTERY EVENT

6:30 p.m.	Guests arrive and check in.
6:50 p.m.	Welcome and introductions.
	Murder is revealed.
	Guests are deputized and rules explained.
	Guests self-select into teams (or go solo) and are given solution sheets.
	Suspects are sent to their positions in library.
7:00 p.m.	Detectives are turned loose to interrogate suspects and look for clues.
8:00 p.m.	Dessert is served.
	Detectives must turn in solution sheets.
	Solution sheets are tallied by staff, and the winning team is selected.
8:15 p.m.	The true plot is revealed.
	Runner-up teams receive prizes.
	The winning team gets the grand prize.
8:30 p.m.	Guests are checked out and go home.
	Library staff and teen group stay to clean up.
9:00 p.m.	Everybody goes home.

Make sure you plan out and practice your big reveal at the end. This is the conclu-sion to the event, and you want it to be as dramatic as possible. It's okay to have a script for this part (see the following example).

Once you have your story and your characters firmly in place, you are good to go. But you don't have to stop there. In the production and the advertising of the event, you can get as creative as you want.

The great thing about an event like this is that it can really incorporate the full spec-trum of the arts. Writing and acting are at the core of creating and hosting a murder mystery event. You need to do those two things to have a successful event. But liter-ally any other aspect of the arts can be layered onto this event to make it even more spectacular. Find out what your teens are into and incorporate it into the event. Do you have a teen who likes to draw? Have them illustrate a poster to advertise your event. If you have a teen who is into costume design, have them create costumes for the different characters. A teen could be in charge of creating a music playlist to set a mood for the event. Film and edit a video advertising the event and put it up on social media. I have had a group of teens who were into making little videos create a pretty awesome short video in the style of a movie preview that we used to advertise a Murder Mystery Event. Whatever your teens are into, they can bring to the table and help enhance the event.

Remember, the golden rule is that everyone should be having fun. Try to always keep that in mind while planning and implementing the event. If you stick with that, it will all turn out well.

STEP-BY-STEP EXAMPLE

We are now going to walk through an example of creating a murder mystery event, step by step. This is based on a real example of a murder mystery event that I worked with a teen group to write and perform. The names and faces have been changed to protect the innocent.

STEP 1: Brainstorm the Victim and the Suspects

After several brainstorming sessions, the teens decided that our murder victim would be Death. Yes, Death, as in the Grim Reaper. It was a meta-idea. It took some additional brainstorming to determine who the suspects would be. At one point it was suggested that God could be a suspect. I hate to be one to squash anyone's creativity, but I rather quickly said we should not be featuring God as a character. It is good to rock the boat sometimes, but it can also be good to avoid controversy when you can. Eventually it was decided that there would be seven suspects and that each one would be the embodiment of one of the Seven Deadly Sins: Sloth, Lust, Anger, Pride, Envy, Greed, and Gluttony.

STEP 2: Create the Setting

Coming up with a context that made some sort of narrative sense for Death and the Seven Deadly Sins to all be hanging out together was a challenge. After more brainstorming, we hit on the idea that Death had a book club that the Seven Deadly Sins all attended. For Halloween, the book club was going to take place at the library, and Death was going to open up the book club to anyone who wanted to attend, hence giving us a logical reason to invite all our guests to this event.

Our story line was that Death and Seven Deadly Sins met early before all the guests arrived to decide on what next month's book club selection would be. While our guests arrived, Death would be in the kitchen working on dessert while all the suspects were at the head table. During the course of the meal, it would be revealed that Death had been murdered and then our guests would be tasked with solving the mystery.

STEP 3: Create Motivations for All the Suspects

The personality traits of the embodiment of the Seven Deadly Sins provided us some obvious motivations for Murder. This is what we decided on:

Sloth—Thought the book club was too much work. Killed Death so they could stop reading books and just watch TV.

Lust—Had an affair with Death. Death ended it because Lust has a history of not being faithful. Lust murdered Death in a jealous rage.

Anger—Wants to kill everybody.

Pride—Death made fun of Pride's suggested book choice for the next book club meeting, Junie B. Jones—said it was a book for kids. Hurt her pride. Pride retaliated by murdering Death.

Envy—Wants to be Death.

Greed—Death owed her money.

Gluttony—Death ate the last cookie, which was too much for poor Gluttony, who flew into an insane rage and murdered Death.

STEP 4: Use the Motivations to Create the True Plot

It was decided that three of the Suspects actually worked together to murder Death: Envy, Greed, and Gluttony. Having multiple guilty parties is a nice little twist. Our detectives may only be looking for one guilty person, so having triple murderers might be a nice surprise. But the real reason the teens decided to have Envy, Greed, and Gluttony be the murderers is, they all thought it was funny that the acronym for the three names was "EGG." We would later use the "EGG" acronym as a pretty big clue.

This is the story we came up with for how it all went down: Envy wants to be the new Death. He thinks Death is so cool and has lots of creepy obsessive fan pictures of Death on his blog. Envy thinks he could be so much better at the job. But he knows he's not strong enough to do it himself. Envy knows Death is way in debt to Greed because of their monthly poker game (the group meets once a month for their book club, once a month to play poker, and once a month for a knitting group). Envy tells Greed he'll pay him the debt with interest once Envy becomes Death, if Greed helps him kill Death. Greed Agrees but decides they need more muscle to be safe and a patsy to pin the murder on. So Greed pockets all the cookies that were for dessert and tells Gluttony that Death ate them all. Gluttony confronts Death in a blind rage; they struggle, and Envy and Greed join in, and all three manage to push Death out the window. They all rush back to the dining room and pretend like nothing happened.

STEP 5: Divide the Plot among All the Suspects

We took the above story and divvied up all the plot points and spread them out among all our suspects. We also ranked everyone's information into three tiers: (1) information suspects would voluntarily share, (2) information they would share only if questioned or pressed, and (3) information that they would desperately try and hide through misdirection or outright lies but might accidentally let slip under the right circumstances. As you will see later, most suspects don't have level 3 information. And that's okay. Detectives will still have to ask the right questions to get the right information.

In order to give everyone meaningful information, we also fleshed out the story to include a subplot about Sloth, Lust, Anger, and Pride starting their own splinter book group called "SLAP" (an acronym of their four names). By drawing attention to the SLAP acronym, it acted as a subtle clue for our detectives to think about what "EGG" might stand for. It was also decided that both Pride and Envy would have blogs that would contain clues to the murder plot.

Another idea that was introduced at this stage was that Death's murdered body would contain significant clues if examined. The primary clue being that after Death was pushed out the kitchen window and fell to her death, she survived long enough to write out the letters *E, G, G* in whip cream before dying.

All the suspects knew the following general information:

The night of the murder, they all met before guests arrived. The group had a big argument over what the next book was going to be. Everyone was mad. They didn't come to a consensus. It's a pretty volatile group and they often fight, but it never really leads to anything. They also meet once a month to play poker. And once a month for a knitting group. Death owed Greed a lot of money in the poker game. At the last game, Death and Greed had a pretty big fight about it. If asked what the "EGG" writing means, all suspects will say Death's favorite food is Eggo Waffles and it was probably her dying wish to have some more Eggo Waffles (but she died before she could write the last letter "o").

This is what each individual Suspect knew:

Sloth
Level 1 Information

Sloth knows about the idea for splinter book club called SLAP; will point to Pride as the starter of the new book club. Sloth thinks Lust murdered Death in a jealous rage after Death ended their affair.

Level 2 Information

If directly asked, Sloth will admit that she did go to the kitchen right before Death was murdered, looking for more food. In the kitchen she saw Greed pocketing all the cookies. Sloth left the kitchen and decided she would just wait until Death finished the other dessert.

Lust
Level 1 Information

Lust knows about the idea for splinter book club called SLAP; will point to Pride as the starter of the new book club. Lust thinks Anger murdered Death. Everyone knows that Anger wants to kill everyone.

Level 2 Information

If directly asked, Lust will reluctantly admit to having had an affair with Death. Lust is really upset that Death ended the affair. If asked, Lust will readily admit to having affairs with everyone in the book club except for Greed and Envy. Lust says that Greed and Envy have always been way too much into each other to even be aware of anyone else. Early that night, Lust overhead them having lovey-dovey talk, something about how Envy was going to make Greed rich once Envy got this new job or something.

Anger
Level 1 Information

Anger knows about the idea for splinter book club called SLAP; will point to Pride as the starter of the new book club. Anger thinks Greed did it. Anger knows Death owed Greed a lot of money and wasn't paying up. Death and the Seven Deadly Sins had a long-running poker game, and Death was a terrible poker player. Death owed Greed tons of money and kept borrowing more from Greed.

Level 2 Information

If Anger is confronted about her rage, she will counter that everyone gets mad sometimes. For example, earlier tonight she saw Gluttony get really mad when Greed told her that Death had eaten all the cookies.

Pride
Level 1 Information

Pride will take every opportunity to brag about her blog and how popular it is. Pride will insist that not one of them could possibly be strong enough to push death out the window. Pride thinks she would be the only one resourceful enough to figure out a way to do it. But obviously she didn't do it. She's above that. Maybe Death couldn't hack it anymore and threw herself out the window.

Level 2 Information

If pressed, Pride will admit to starting a splinter book club called SLAP with his favorite people in the group. Pride doesn't really have anything against Death, Envy, Greed, and Gluttony. She doesn't particularly like any of them. If asked directly about Envy's blog, pride will snub it and say it's a pale imitation of her much more superior blog. If asked about Death snubbing Pride's choice for next month's book club book, Pride will get very haughty and refuse to talk about the subject.

Envy
Level 1 Information

Envy is really jealous about SLAP. He read about it on Pride's blog. Envy blames SLAP for murder. He will say he thinks the four of them worked together to murder Death so they could start their own book club. They are probably planning on murdering Envy, Greed, and Gluttony too to get rid of all the book club competition.

Level 2 Information

If asked why he reacted the way he did when the new Death appeared, Envy will say he was just surprised to learn that the Universe automatically created a new Death upon the death of the old Death. He didn't know it worked that way. He thought there might a job posting and interviews for the new Death. If accused of the murder with substantial proof, Envy will turn on Gluttony and say he saw Gluttony push him out the window, after falling into a blind rage after finding out that Death had eaten all the cookies. Envy says he tried to stop Gluttony but couldn't hold her back.

Level 3 Information

Under no circumstances will Envy admit to being behind the murder. But Envy will let it slip that he thinks he would be a much better Death given the opportunity.

Greed
Level 1 Information

Greed will say he thinks Pride committed the murder. Death made fun of Pride's book choice for next month, Junie B. Jones. Death hurt her pride.

Level 2 Information

If accused of the murder with substantial proof, Greed will turn on Gluttony and say he saw Gluttony push him out the window, after falling into a blind rage after finding out that Death had eaten all the cookies. Greed says he tried to stop Gluttony but couldn't hold her back.

Level 3 Information

Greed will not admit to plotting the murder with Envy or taking all the cookies or telling Gluttony that Death ate all the cookies. Greed will lie about all those things. Greed will even deny that there are cookies in his pockets, when a casual inspection will show that his pockets are bulging with them.

Gluttony
Level 1 Information

Gluttony saw Sloth get up off the couch (which was a really unusual event in and of itself) and go into the kitchen right before Death was murdered. Gluttony will say she thinks Sloth was too lazy to read books for book club, so she killed Death to end the book club.

Level 2 Information

If the cookies get brought up at all, Gluttony will go crazy and start screaming incoherently but is too upset about the cookies to really answer any questions about them. If it is revealed to Gluttony that Greed has pockets full of cookies, Gluttony will scream like a maniac and swear vengeance on Greed for taking the cookies.

Level 3 Information

Gluttony thinks she killed Death all by herself. She doesn't realize that she was manipulated by Greed and Pride. She was in such a rage when she attacked Death that she doesn't actually know that Pride and Greed also pushed Death out the window. She honestly thinks Pride and Greed may have tried to stop her.

STEP 6: Create Physical Clues

Relying on physical clues can be tricky because you don't want participants to pick them up and take them and not allow other participants access. If the actual murder scene with a body is a clue (as is the case in this example with Death's body), you can put police tape around the body and instruct participants that they can investigate but cannot touch anything surrounded by police tape. You can also make multiple copies of items you want multiple participants to find. In the past, we've used fake newspaper articles, of which we made multiple copies and spread throughout the library so they would be easy for lots of teams to find. In this example, we took a more modern approach and created two blogs that contained clues. Advertisements for the characters' blogs were posted throughout the library, with the web address displayed prominently. We even wrote the blog web addresses on the bottoms of plates that we served the food on. The idea was that detectives could look up the blogs on their smartphones or use computers that were on and available in the library.

PHYSICAL CLUE #1: Death's Body

Just outside of the room that we all ate dinner in was the body of Death. We borrowed a skeleton from a local school's science classroom, dressed it in a black robe, and gave it a plastic sickle. One finger was posed outstretched with whipped cream on the tip. The letters *E G G* were spelled out on the ground in whipped cream. Several small hard candies were scattered about the scene (the character of Gluttony was eating from a stash of the same hard candies throughout the night). On inspection, one could also see faint red-and-green fingerprints on Death's black robe. The red-and-green colors matched the red-and-green gelatin that was on Envy and Greed's plates, respectively.

PHYSICAL CLUE #2: Pride's Blog

Using a simple Google Doc, we made a serviceable fake blog. We went to tinyurl. com and created a manageable URL shortcut. All of the teens involved in the writing process of the murder mystery took turns writing different entries in Pride's blog.

Figure 3.2 Some examples of the "creepy fan art" we used to populate Envy's obsessive blog.

We treated it like a creative writing challenge. They could write whatever they wanted that was in the character of Pride. We also populated the fake blog with pictures and animated gifs (including lots of selfies). Buried within the blog entries were several clues to our murder mystery plot. Not all of the clues were important to solving the mystery, but they did all help round out the larger story. Pride's Blog included references to how much Pride wanted Junie B. Jones to be the next choice for the book club. There was also some writing expressing disappointment with how Death was running the book club and a desire to start a new book club with just Sloth, Lust, Anger, and Pride, called the SLAP Book Club. There's also some mention of how clingy Envy and Greed have become and speculation as to the nature of their relationship.

PHYSICAL CLUE #3: Envy's Blog

We also created a fake blog for Envy, using the same method as Pride's blog. The overall theme of this blog was Envy's obsession with Death. There were lots of creepy obsessive Death fan art (see Figure 3.2), as well as long-winded musings about what it would be like to be Death. There were positive things written about Greed and Gluttony, and resentful posts about all the other Seven Deadly Sins. Buried in the blog was the idea of starting a new book club in retaliation to the SLAP Book Club, but Envy was having a hard time coming up with a good name. The best Envy could think of was the GEG Book Club.

ADDITIONAL PHYSICAL CLUES

There were also some small physical clues that supported other evidence. These included the small candies Gluttony had on hand that matched the candies found on Death's body, the red-and-green gelatin on Greed and Gluttony's plates, and the cookies that were stuffed in Greed's pockets.

BRAINSTORMING CHECKLIST

☐ Murder victim
☐ Suspects
☐ Setting
☐ Suspects' motivations
☐ True plot
☐ Physical clues

STEP 7: Practice, Practice, Practice

We spent a lot of meetings practicing being in character. The teens took turns playing the part of the detectives and grilling the suspects. There is no script for the characters because you can't anticipate every possible question a suspect might be asked. But what you can do is really practice being in character. If teens revealed things they shouldn't have under questioning or failed to reveal things they should have, it was commented on and practiced more.

We did write scripts for the Introduction we used to greet our guests at the beginning of the night and the Conclusion we used to wrap up the event (see the following sample scripts). Both of those performances did not require much audience interaction and could be practiced and performed in a scripted manner. That being said, we weren't slaves to the script. Writing the script was more an exercise in getting all the relevant information we needed to impart on the page. In rehearsing, a lot of the wording of the script was changed, but we worked to make sure we stayed true to the content of our script and that we didn't leave out anything critical to our story.

While we were practicing, it was up to the teens to assemble costumes for each of their characters. We also spent time staging the borrowed science classroom skeleton we used for the crime scene and gathering any other supplies we might need.

STEP 8: Advertise

Writing, preparing, and rehearsing your murder mystery event can be a ton of fun. But don't forget to advertise the event as well. After all, you will need detectives to show up to try and solve the mystery. Do what you can for advertising. Print some posters (see Figure 3.3) to advertise in-house in the library or put them up around your community. Have the teens who wrote and are performing the murder mystery invite their friends. Give them fliers to put up in their schools. Use social media. Doing an interactive murder mystery event for teens in the library is a novel enough program that you should get some decent word-of-mouth advertising, and hopefully you will pack it out.

Figure 3.3. This is the image we used to advertise the event. The date, time, and all relevant details were superimposed over the art, along with a brief statement explaining that this was a Halloween-themed event and participants were encouraged to come dressed in costumes.

STEP 9: Do It!

So we did it. And it went well. We were at capacity with about 50 teenagers running around the library and having a good time. I will say that no single group uncovered every single detail of the murder plot. But several teams deduced that Envy, Greed, and Gluttony committed the murder together and that Envy was the ringleader. The team that turned in their answer sheet first with the most accurate deduction was declared the champion. Incidentally, the team that won was a duo who also came in second place in our costume contest. They named their team "Heaven and Hell." One teen was dressed as an angel and the other as a devil—very appropriate costumes for the theme of our murder mystery event.

Sample Introduction Script

HOST:

Hello. Thank you, all, for joining us for Death's book club meeting tonight at the library. My name is Dante; I'm a librarian here. I hope you all read this month's selection, The Magic Tree House #666: Inside the Inferno. We will start our book discussion in just a few minutes. But first a couple of announcements: Next week we have our monthly poker game, and the week after that is the monthly Knitting circle. I hope you will all join us for both of those meetings as well.

I would like to introduce our book club board members: Sloth, Lust, Anger, Pride, Envy, Greed, and Gluttony.

And, of course, there is our book club president, Death. Death at the moment is back in the kitchen, currently working on dessert. As you may or may not know, Death is quite the gourmet and is whipping up something super special to serve along with the wonderful cookies Gluttony was kind enough to share with us tonight.

(GLUTTONY reacts at the mention of the cookies, howling in agony and hiding her face.)
HOST:

As you can see, sharing desserts isn't something Gluttony is accustomed to. But she's trying. So let's all let her know how much we like the cookies when they come out later.

(Enter DEATH)

DEATH:

Murder!

HOST:

Excuse me?

DEATH:

Murder!

HOST:

There's been a murder? But, pray, say who has been murdered!

DEATH:

Me.

HOST:

Come again?

DEATH:

I have been murdered.

HOST:

But how can that be? You are standing here before us.

DEATH:

I am the new incarnation of Death. Death is eternal. But my predecessor was murdered. That is why I have arrived.

ENVY:

The Universe just created a new Death?

(GREED shoots ENVY a very angry look.)
DEATH:

Indeed.

HOST:

So Death has been murdered? Oh, the irony! I can hardly take it! But tell us, new Death, when was the old Death murdered and how?

DEATH:

I retain some of the memories of my predecessor but they are incomplete. The details of the murder are a mystery to me. But I do know that Death was murdered exactly 30 minutes ago here in the library.

HOST:

30 minutes ago? That means one of the Seven must have murdered Death! One of these (indicating the seven suspects at the head table) sinful people must have done the heinous deed right before the rest of you all came in.

With the power vested in me as a librarian, I'm deputizing you all as detectives and asking for your help in solving this mystery. You can work by yourself or break up into teams as you see fit.

All seven of our suspects will be confined to the library and made available to be interviewed. I would also invite you to investigate the body of death for clues. But please do not actually touch the body. After all, it is evidence. You may also search the rest of the library for more clues. It is Halloween, so there may even be candy hidden about—who knows . . .

You must discover three things: Who committed the murder? Why did they do it? And how did they commit the act? Once you think you have solved the mystery, turn in your paperwork to me or any other library staff member. The individual or team who solves the mystery the most accurately in the least amount of time will be declared the winner!

You have until 8:00, when we shall reconvene here in this room for dessert. Now go! Go! Go! And bring us justice for poor old Death!

Sample Conclusion Script

HOST:

We have gone over your answer sheets, and I am pleased to announce that with your help, we were able to solve the mystery of who murdered Death. Let's quickly go over what we have all learned in the course of our investigations.

(HOST walks down the head table indicating each subject one at a time).
HOST:

Was it Death? Did Death commit suicide by throwing herself out the window? No, Death did not commit suicide.

Was it Sloth? Sloth, who is so lazy that she might just rather end the book club by murdering Death instead of having to read another book? Sloth, who was seen entering the kitchen shortly before Death's murder? No, it was not Sloth. Sloth did go into the kitchen looking for cookies . . . but someone had taken them all!

Was it Lust? It was well known that Lust and Death had an affair that ended very badly when Death dumped Lust. Did Lust murder Death in a jealous rage? No, Lust did not murder Death. Lust has had affairs with everyone; he is lust after all . . . In fact, there are just two members of the book club that Lust hasn't had an affair with. Two members who were too into each other to pay Lust any mind at all . . .

Was it Anger? Anger certainly has the rage and blood lust to commit murder. And Anger pretty much hates everyone. But it wasn't Anger. Everyone gets angry after all. In fact, Anger saw someone get really upset earlier in the night when it was revealed that all of the cookies had been eaten . . .

What about Pride? It is true that Death hurt Pride's pride when Death belittled Pride's choice of Junie B. Jones for next week's book club selection. But the question is, was Pride's pride hurt enough to cause her to fly into a murderous rage and throw poor Death out a window? . . . No. The answer is no. Pride did not murder Death. Despite Pride's assertions that she was the only member of the book club smart enough to single-handedly pull off such a feat as to murder Death itself. And Pride was right! Death was not murdered by a single member of the book club . . .

What about Gluttony? Gluttony who was so upset about all of the cookies being eaten that Gluttony flew into a blind rage and did . . . and did what exactly?

GLUTTONY:

I did it! I murdered Death! I admit it! Death ate all the cookies!

HOST:

Yes, yes, you did. But you were not acting alone!

GLUTTONY:

I wasn't?

HOST:

No! You were being manipulated by others. You were set up to enact the murder and take the fall. It was the perfect crime. But it wasn't really you behind it all. Death did not eat all the cookies! Greed stole them all and then told you that Death had eaten the cookies!

GLUTTONY (enraged):

What?

HOST:

Greed set you up. Greed, whom Death owed lots and lots of money. Death was in debt to Greed from the monthly poker game. Greed, who thought she was going to get that money back when the new Death took over. Greed, who thought the new Death would be Greed's lover . . .

Envy! Envy, who is obsessed with Death! Envy, who runs a super-creepy blog filled with obsessive Death fan art on it. Envy, who wanted to be Death so bad, she concocted a murder scheme with her lover Greed, and they got Gluttony to do the dirty work!

And there you have it! The three of them together murdered Death. It was Envy, Greed, and Gluttony, also known as E G G, who are guilty of this heinous crime!

And thanks to you fine detectives, we were able to solve this mystery. Many of you solved it correctly, or nearly correctly. But the winners are the team that solved the mystery the most accurately in the least amount of time . . .

EXAMPLES OF DIFFERENT LIBRARY MURDER MYSTERY EVENTS

Who Murdered Waldo?

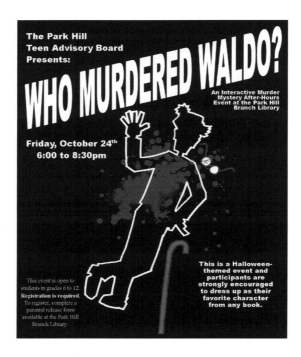

The premise of the event was that we were having a dinner at the library to honor Waldo for his contributions to literature. Seated at the head table with Waldo were other literary guests of honor, including Sherlock Holmes, Batman, Odlaw, Enola Holmes, and others. During the course of the dinner, the lights suddenly went out, and there was a bloodcurdling scream. When the lights came back on, Waldo was dead. Everyone seated at the head table was a suspect.

Spoiler Alert: It was Sherlock Holmes. He murdered Waldo because he was just too hard to find in all the books, and it tormented Sherlock's logical brain.

When teens signed up for the event, they were given invitations to the dinner honoring Waldo for his contributions to literature. On the back side of the invitation was a piece of evidence that hinted that murder was in the air.

Who Murdered Alice?

At a mad tea-party-style dinner to celebrate Alice's unbirthday, the mood goes from jovial to deadly serious when it is discovered that Alice has been murdered. The Queen of Hearts, the Dormouse, the Mad Hatter, the Cheshire Cat, Tweedle Dee, and Tweedle Dum are all suspects.

The Sam Gary Branch Library
Teen Advisory Board
Presents An Interactive
Murder Mystery
After-Hours
Event:

WHO MURDERED ALICE?
A WONDERLAND MYSTERY
Friday, October 16th 6:30 to 8:30pm
Solve The Mystery!
Win Prizes!

This event is open to students in grades 6 to 12. **Registration is required.** To register, complete a parental release form available at the Sam Gary Branch Library.

This is a Halloween-themed event and participants are strongly encouraged to dress up as their favorite character from any book.

Spoiler Alert: It was the Dormouse. But it was an accident. He poisoned the Queen's dessert, meaning to murder her in revenge for her ruthless efforts to eradicate vermin from the land, which resulted in the Dormouse's whole family being wiped out. But Tweedle Dee and Tweedle Dum mixed up the dessert plates and accidentally served Alice the poisoned dessert.

Newspapers reporting the great rodent massacre of Wonderland were lying around the library to provide clues. As were empty bottles of poison.

Who Murdered Willy Wonka?

To celebrate 10 years of successful business together, Charlie and Willy Wonka had a feast at the chocolate factory. The original contestants were invited to return to the factory for a recreation of their historic tour. Following the tour, there was a ban-

Who Murdered Willy Wonka?
A CHOCOLATE FACTORY MYSTERY

quet with more guests. At dessert time, Willy Wonka made his grand entrance in his flying glass elevator (in actuality, made of PVC pipe and Saran Wrap and suspended by ropes and pulleys). But then something went horribly wrong. The elevator crashed, and poor Willy Wonka died. But this was no accident. The glass elevator was sabotaged!

Augustus Gloop was suspiciously missing from the dinner. When our detectives investigated the murder, they followed chocolate footprints from the lake of chocolate to the bathroom. When they opened the door to the bathroom, there were shrieks of startled horror as they discovered a second body, Augustus Gloop, slumped over dead on the toilet. It was a double murder!

Spoiler Alert: It was Violet Beauregarde and Veruca Salt working together to get revenge on Willy Wonka for not giving them the chocolate factory 10 years ago. They had sabotaged the glass elevator (which of course runs on chocolate) by stuffing it full of vegetables. And when Augustus Gloop saw them doing it, they drowned him in the chocolate lake and then tried to hide his body in the toilet.

CHAPTER FOUR

ANIMATION
MAKING THINGS MOVE

WALT DISNEY FAMOUSLY ONCE SAID, "IF YOU CAN DREAM IT, YOU CAN DO IT." HE WAS TALKING ABOUT ANIMATION, AND HE WAS RIGHT. ANYTHING YOU CAN IMAGINE YOU CAN MAKE WITH ANIMATION. AND BECAUSE ANIMATION "MOVES," IT BECOMES, IN A SENSE, REAL. ANIMATION IS AN INCREDIBLE ART FORM WITH LIMITLESS POSSIBILITIES.

MOST PEOPLE ASSOCIATE ANIMATION WITH FILM. BUT HISTORICALLY SPEAKING, ANIMATION PREDATES THE INVENTION OF FILM. ANIMATED FILMS AND CARTOONS ARE WONDERFUL IN THEIR OWN RIGHT, BUT THERE ARE MUCH MORE ACCESSIBLE AND IMMEDIATE ANIMATION TECHNIQUES THAT CAN EASILY BE COMPLETED WITH A MINIMUM OF SUPPLIES IN A SHORT TIME.

THE THAUMATROPE AND ZOETROPE ARE VICTORIAN-ERA WONDERS THAT DAZZLED AUDIENCES OF ADULTS AND CHILDREN ALIKE. SOME PEOPLE LIKEN ANIMATED GIFS TO THE MODERN DIGITAL EQUIVALENT OF THESE CLASSICAL ANIMATION TECHNIQUES.

IN 1868, JOHN BARNES LINNETT PATENTED A NEW INVENTION HE CALLED THE KINEOGRAPH. THAT WAS THE FIRST FLIP BOOK. FLIP BOOKS ARE COMPOSED OF STILL IMAGES THAT APPEAR TO MOVE WHEN VIEWED IN QUICK SUCCESSION. ALL ANIMATION WORKS ON THAT SIMPLE PRINCIPLE. ANIMATION IS THE ILLUSION OF MOVEMENT. ANY FILM YOU SEE (ANIMATED OR LIVE ACTION) ON ANY SCREEN (IN THE MOVIE THEATER OR ON YOUR SMARTPHONE) DOESN'T REALLY MOVE. IT IS A RAPID SUCCESSION OF IMAGES THAT CREATES THE ILLUSION OF MOVEMENT.

WHEN THE BIG BRAINS AT LIFELONG KINDERGARTEN GROUP AT THE MIT MEDIA LAB CREATED THE OPEN SOURCE PROGRAM SCRATCH, THEY GAVE THE WORLD FREE ACCESS TO A SIMPLISTIC YET POWERFUL PROGRAM THAT ALLOWS ANYONE TO MAKE INTERACTIVE ANIMATIONS OR VIDEO GAMES.

ALL OF THESE ANIMATION TECHNIQUES ARE EASY TO MASTER AND CAN PRODUCE QUICK, SATISFYING RESULTS WITH JUST A LITTLE BIT OF PRACTICE.

THAUMATROPE

Thaumatrope is Greek for "Turning Marvel." A thaumatrope is usually a disk with an image on either side. Perhaps the best-known thaumatrope is the classic image of a bird on one side of the disk and an empty cage on the other. By punching a hole on either side of the disk and tying a string to both ends, users can twist up the thaumatrope and then spin it. When the disks rapidly flip over, the two images will merge to the naked eye, creating a single image of a bird in a cage. It's a fun visual illusion courtesy of a phenomenon known as "the persistence of vision." But it's not really animation.

However, exactly the same method can be used to create a simple animation. Instead of using a disk, a simple rectangle of paper will work even better. Fold the rectangle in half to create a square, and then draw a two-step animation on both sides.

A two-step animation is a sequence that has only two separate parts but can be repeated indefinitely. A bat flapping its wings up and then down is a good example of a two-step animation. You could also have a stick figure standing on the ground, then jumping into the air. Or a face with the eyebrows up, then the eyebrows down. You get the idea.

Once you have both steps drawn—one onto each side of your square of paper—you need to attach some sort of stick. Open the folded rectangle and insert a thin wooden dowel (or a pencil or a pen will work just as well) inside the fold. Tape or glue the stick to one side of the rectangle, close the fold, and tape or glue the bottom edge. Then start spinning your stick and, voila! You have created an amazing animation. It may not seem like much, but trust me, if you showed this to a caveman, they would freak out. Then they would probably burn you for being a witch. But it would have been worth it because you would have blown their primordial mind.

This is animation at its simplest. Two separate images viewed in rapid succession to create the illusion of movement. All animation follows this simple principle.

ZOETROPE

If doing the two-step with the thaumatrope isn't doing it for you anymore, it might be time to start adding some more steps. That's where the zoetrope comes in. Zoetrope is Greek for "the Wheel of Life." The original name of the device was the "Dædaleum" which very roughly translates as the "Wheel of the Devil." But then some clever Victorian-era marketer realized they might do better if they didn't associate their toy with devil worship, and so it became the zoetrope and the name stuck.

The zoetrope operates using the same principle as the thaumatrope, but instead of just having two steps, there are multiple steps to create a more fluid animation. The steps are drawn in a sequence on a slip of paper. The paper is inserted into a hollow drum with regularly cut slits in the side. The drum is spun on an axis, and then by looking into the slits, you can view an amazing animation sequence.

You can buy a decent zoetrope at a toy store for about $15. They come with several sample animation strips, including the obligatory zoetrope horse-racing animation. And usually there will be a few blank strips provided to create your own custom animations. If not, you can always make your own animation strips with a blank piece of paper.

If you are really cheap, or if you're running a workshop and you want all your participants to walk out with their own zoetrope, it may be more economical to build your own zoetrope. A store-bought zoetrope is bound to create a smoother animation, but a simple drum constructed from cardstock with a slit cut into it spun on a dowel will produce a similar effect. Paper, scissors, glue, and access to a computer and a printer is all you need to make your own zoetrope.

If you search "zoetrope template" on the internet, you can find a variety of print-ready templates that can be copied onto cardstock and cut out to create your own zoetrope. A thin, smooth wooden dowel will make good axis for a homemade zoetrope but a simple pencil will also suffice. Size matters. The larger the zoetrope you construct, the more steps you can add to your animation and the more fluid the resulting animation will be.

The real beauty of the zoetrope is that it is a three-dimensional object that you interact with physically to create an animation. It is a great hands-on activity for students to engage with that will teach them about animation without ever looking at a screen.

Whether you buy a zoetrope or construct your own, you should absolutely have your students create their own original animation strips. Put them in the zoetrope, give that sucker a spin, and marvel at the "Wheel of Life" in action.

FLIP BOOK

The Flip Book is a common animation technique in which a user flips through a series of pages illustrated with animation steps to create the illusion of movement. If you haven't noticed already, this very book you are holding in your hands contains a flip book in the lower left-hand corner. By rapidly flipping through the pages of this book, you can animate the sequence. If you flip backward, you can run the animation in reverse.

You can deface the corner pages of any book with little drawings to make a flip book. Or you can use a small notepad. Small, blank notepads work the best. Post-It Notes will work, but in my experience, pads of Post-It Notes tend to split after multiple flippings. I would recommend using small blank memo pads that are perfect bound at the top (as opposed to spiral bound).

Always practice flipping before you start drawing. Only a portion of the corner of any pad will be visible while you are flipping. Take care that your illustrations don't stretch out past the realm of visibility.

As far as drawing implements go, a pencil usually works the best. You will want to draw with something dark enough (but not too dark) that that it is barely visible through one sheet of your pad. Draw your first step on the bottom sheet of your pad, holding the rest of the pages up. Lower one sheet and look through it at the "ghost" of the previous step. Using the ghost as a guide, draw your next step. The key to creating a nice smooth flip book animation is to only have tiny changes between your steps. Keep in mind, each separate step will only last the briefest fraction of a second.

Flip books are a lot of fun, but it takes a lot of drawing to create just a few seconds of animation. In my experience, most teens don't have the stamina to draw more than a very short flip book animation. Drawing a flip book animation can also be a very solitary activity without much social interaction. A way to overcome both of those obstacles is to do an Animation Jam Flip Book workshop.

Creating an Animation Jam is easy. All it requires is that each participant starts and stops their flip book with the same image. It works best if you draw the same image on the first page of each flip book. I typically draw a small circle in the bottom left-hand corner. I then instruct the teens that they can do whatever they want with that circle over the course of their flipbook. They can make the circle race across the page. They can make the circle shrink or grow. They can morph the circle into a killer robot that flies off into outer space to do battle with a gigantic spider on Neptune's moon. They can really do whatever they want with the circle. The only rule is that they have to end their flip book sequence with an identical circle back in the same spot in the lower left-hand corner. This is a great project because it is completely up to each individual teen how long and involved they want each of their flip book animations to be.

Once the teens have finished with their flip books, you collect them. If some stragglers haven't finished theirs, it's on you to finish drawing the flip books to get them to end with a circle back at the starting point. Then you film each flip book with whatever camera you have on hand. If you take care to line up each flip book in the same place in your camera's frame, the beginning circle and the ending circle should all be in the same place. Using some simple video-editing software (the standard Mac-based iMovie or Windows-based Movie Maker video-editing programs will work just fine), splice all the animations together. What you'll end up with is an awesome and bizarre Animation Jam that's one fluid animation. For added awesomeness, add some music to your video. Music makes everything better.

ANIMATED GIFS

The internet was invented so people could share cute cat pictures. That's a fact. Cute cat pictures are the pinnacle of modern technology. But what's even better than a cute cat picture? How about a cute cat picture that moves! Everyone loves animated gifs. I had to do a lot of painstaking research to write this book, including watching lots and lots of animated gifs on the internet. As I'm writing this, I just found one animated gif that is a loop of a kitten squeezing itself in and out of a little brown paper bag. And let me tell you, there's a good chance I might not finish this book now. The rest of the pages from here on out might be blank, because I don't want to do anything at all except watch this animated gif, forever.

. . . Okay, obviously there is more in this book. So, yes, I did eventually stop watching that animated gif and (reluctantly) get on with my life. I tried to convince my editor to insert about 10 blank pages after that last sentence to really make it plausible that we might just stop the book at this point. But the publisher wouldn't go for it.

The point I'm trying to make is that animated gifs are magic. A good animated gif is mesmerizing. You don't ever want to stop looking at it. But all an animated gif is, really, the modern digital equivalent of a simple animation device like zoetrope. An animated gif is just a sequence of images viewed in rapid succession to create the illusion of movement. And they are easy to make.

Making an animated gif does require access to a computer. But all the necessary software involved in creating the animated gif can be downloaded for free off the internet.

First you will need digital imaging software that will allow you to save files in the. gif format. Back in Chapter Two: Graphic Novel Creation, I extolled the virtues of paint.net. Go back and read that part again if you forgot. Or if you're one of those lazy people who only reads bits and pieces in books, and you skipped over Part Two and have no intention of going back and reading it, you'll just have to take my word for it: paint.net is great.

You can download paint.net at https://www.getpaint.net. Do not go to www.paint .net. www.paint.net is the website for a house paint manufacturer. I'm sure they make perfectly nice house paint, but that's not what we're interested in right now. Go to https://www.getpaint.net and follow instructions to download the latest version of the program paint.net. Read through the website carefully and make sure you are clicking on the correct button to download the correct software. Paint.net is reliable, safe software to download onto your computer. But unfortunately there are questionable advertisers who buy ad space on the getpaint.net website and create misleading ads that are meant to look like the download buttons that try to trick you into downloading all kinds of crap you don't want that might be harmful to your computer. So pay attention to what you click on.

Once you have digital imaging software capable of saving files in the .gif format, you will need more software to convert those files into an animated gif. I recommend using UnFREEz. It is extremely simple, easy-to-use software that takes up practically no space at all on your computer. You can download it at http://www.whitsoftdev .com/unfreez/. UnFREEz is a safe, reliable program, but again, read carefully and pay attention to what exactly you are clicking on when you download it.

Using these two programs, you can easily make your own animated gifs. Let's make one together right now, shall we? If you need help with the basics of using paint.net, go back and read through the step-by-step tutorial in Appendix I—Using Paint.net: A Quick and Easy Introduction to Digital Art.

STEP 1: Make Your Canvas
Open up paint.net. From the **File** menu, select **New**. In the **New** pop-up box, set the width and height to 72 pixels; this will create an image that is 1" × 1" on a computer screen.

STEP 2: Create an Eyeball

Click on the **Shape** tool and select the *Ellipse* option to create a circle in the middle of your canvas. Draw a second circle inside the first. Using the **Paint Bucket** tool, fill in the center circle with black and the outer circle with a color. If you want to get fancy, use some white to create a reflection on the eyeball.

STEP 3: Create an Eyelid

From the **Layer** menu, select **Add New Layer** to create a second layer. You'll want to start naming your layers to help differentiate between them. Double click on each layer to access the **Layer Properties**. Rename the Background layer as "Eyeball" and Layer 2 as "Eyelid." While the Eyelid layer is selected, using the **Paintbrush** or the **Line/Curve** tool, draw an open eyelid around the eyeball. Use the **Paint Bucket** tool to fill in the outside of the eyelid with a solid color. Decorate the outside of your eye as you see fit, with eyelashes or freckles or whatever; just don't cover up the eyeball.

STEP 4: Create the Frames of Your Animation

Save your image as a paint.net file (.pdn extension) to have as a backup. Then from the File menu, select Save As, rename the file as "Frame 1," and save the file as a gif (.gif extension). Save the file in a folder somewhere where you can easily access it later. Gif files do not support multiple layers. You will be asked to flatten your images. That's okay. Flatten your image. If you ever need to, you can go back to the .pdn file you saved as a backup. After you have saved it as a .gif, go into your History tool and select whatever you did right before you flattened the image. That will un-flatten the image. Then select the Eyeball layer and use the **Move Selected Pixels** tool to move the eye just a little bit. From the **File** menu, select **Save As**, rename the file as "Frame 2," and save the file as a gif (.gif extension).

STEP 5: Repeat as Necessary

Repeat Step 4, over and over, slightly moving the Eyeball and re-saving as a gif with a different name each time. Move the eyeball all around but have it return almost to its starting position before you stop. It is important to have it almost return to the beginning so that when the animation loops, it's a smooth transition from last frame to first frame; otherwise, you'll end up with a very choppy animation. Like with all other animation techniques, the more steps you provide and the slighter the difference between each step, the smoother the final animation will be.

STEP 6: Animate Your Frames

Open UnFREEz. Open the folder where you stored all the gif animation frame files. Drag all the files onto the **Frames** window. Under **Option**s, set the *Frame delay* to 5 cs. You can adjust this later if your animation is running too slow or too fast, but 5 cs is usually the ideal frame delay. Then click on **Make Animated GIF** and save your file. Open your animated gif in any web browser and marvel at its magic.

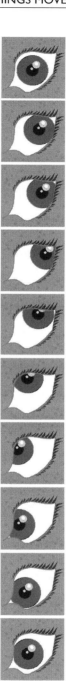

Figure 4.1

STOP-MOTION ANIMATION AND CLAYMATION

Stop-motion animation is an animation technique that involves the physical manipulation of objects that are photographed at different stages. When the photographs are viewed in a rapid sequence, it creates the illusion of movement.

Articulated toys such as dolls or action figures are often used in stop-motion animation because they can be easily posed for photographs. Clay is also a common material to manipulate in stop-motion animation. Clay-based animation is sometimes referred to as Claymation. But really any object can be used. If you choose, you can move rocks around and photograph them in a sequence to create a stop-motion animation. Real, live human beings can be photographed and used to create very interesting stop-motion animations.

Any device that has a camera can be used for stop-motion animation. If you're a hardcore analog artist, you could print photographs and flip through them to create a stop-motion flip book. But if you want to make it easy on yourself, you can always use some sort of video-editing software.

There are a plethora of stop-motion apps available for smartphones and tablets. They all more or less work the same, allowing you to take photographs and load them directly into editing software that sequences the still images into a video. The better stop-motion apps will allow you to adjust your frame rate to increase or decrease your speed. They will also allow you to add music to your film and/or record voice-over to narrate your film.

Using an app is the simplest way to create a stop-motion animation, but any free video-editing software on any platform will also work. You just need to load your pictures into the video-editing program. It is definitely more time consuming to do it that way, but it may also result in giving you more options as to how to craft your film in the end.

SCRATCH

Scratch is a great program for creating animation. You can even take it a step further and create interactive animations, also known as video games. And like all great things in life, Scratch is absolutely free and does not require downloading anything. You do need an e-mail address to sign up for a Scratch account, but if you are an educator (and librarians count as educators), you can sign up for a Scratch Teacher Account. This will allow you to create accounts for your students in advance of any workshop you might be planning.

Scratch can be found at https://scratch.mit.edu. It was developed by MIT and is maintained through grants and donations. Scratch is essentially an online program that allows users to create interactive animations using pre-written bits of code that are snapped together like building blocks to create lines of code. The program was originally developed to teach coding to a target audience of students ranging from 8 to 16 years old. But Scratch is both simple and sophisticated enough to appeal a very wide range of ages and abilities.

In Scratch lingo, the images you animate are called "Sprites." You can import your own artwork into Scratch as a Sprite and animate it. Or you can create Sprites in Scratch using the built-in drawing tools. Or you can simply select preexisting Sprites from the Scratch Library and animate those. The latter is a terrific option if you have students who are reluctant to create their own art but are still interested in animation.

I am not going to devote much more space of this book to explaining all the ins and outs of Scratch. There are plenty of books out there that tackle teaching Scratch to different age groups. There are even more instructional videos available online that will teach anything you'd like to know about Scratch. The Scratch website, https:// scratch.mit.edu, is perhaps the best resource out there for teaching scratch, as it is packed with tutorials, project cards, and teacher guides. In addition, all finished projects that are published on Scratch allow you to "see inside" at the code and Sprites used to create them. So students can learn by imitation as well.

That being said, for the benefit of those who might be hesitant to embark on any endeavor that involves the word "coding," I will go step by step through how to create the simplest of animations in Scratch. It's really easy. Here we go . . .

STEP 1: Go to Scratch
Go to https://scratch.mit.edu. Click on **Create** in the upper left-hand corner, right next to the Scratch logo. If you want to save your progress, you'll need to sign up for an account. But if you're just trying it out, you don't even need to sign up to create something.

STEP 2: Get Rid of the Cat
New projects appear with the Scratch Cat Sprite preloaded. But we're allergic to cats, so we're going to get rid of it. Right click on the Sprite and select **delete**.

STEP 3: Get a New Sprite
In the Sprite workspace, click on the cat head in the lower right-hand corner to *Choose a Sprite* from the library. In the sprite library, find and click on the *Rocketship*.

STEP 4: Code the Sprite
In the **Code** menu, select the *Events* category and click on and drag the brown "when GREEN FLAG clicked" bit of code to the right and into the work space.

In the **Code** menu, select the *Motion* category and click on the blue "go to x: CIRCLE y: CIRCLE" bit of code. Drag that blue piece of code to the right and into the work space, positioning it just below the brown piece of code. Once it is in position, it will "snap into place" on its own.

Inside the blue piece of code, click on the white circles to the right of the x: and type "0." Click on the white circle to the right of the y: and type "-100." This line of code will position the rocket in place at the start of our animation.

In the **Code** menu, select the *Motion* category and click on and drag the blue "glide CIRCLE secs to x: CIRCLE y: CIRCLE" bit of code to the right and into the work space, and snap it into place below the brown piece of code.

Inside that line of script type "1" for the secs, "0" for x:, and "100" for y:.

Congratulations, you just wrote code for a simple animation! Click on the GREEN FLAG and watch it go. The CIRCLES in your code are variables. Change the values and see what happens.

Pretty easy, right? That took, what? A minute? Two minutes? With a few more minutes of work, you could add a background, add sounds, or create a flaming rocket animation coming out of the base of your rocket ship. You could change the controls so that the rocket ship follows the mouse pointer across the screen or goes in the direction of whatever arrow key is pressed on the keyboard. You could make the rocket ship shoot lasers when you press the spacebar. You could create asteroids that hurl at random patterns across the screen and explode when you shoot them with your laser. You could add a scoreboard and tally up points for every asteroid you blow up. You can add enemy spaceships that are trying to blow you up. You can add a health meter that shows you can take three hits from enemies before you blow up. All that and more can be done easily in Scratch.

As I mentioned earlier, if you are looking for more resources, there are plenty of books our there dedicated to teaching Scratch that are geared at specific ages, as well as online tutorials at https://scratch.mit.edu and other places throughout the web. But the best way to become proficient at Scratch is to play around in the program. All published projects on Scratch have a blue button in the upper right-hand corner labeled "See inside" (see Figure 4.1). By clicking on that button, you can open up the work space for that project and see exactly how many sprites and scripts it took to create that project. You can also save a copy of that project and get inside to mess around with it (or "remix" as they say in Scratch lingo). It's fun. It's easy. So get in there and play around. Go make something awesome and then teach some teens how to do the same.

...AND THAT'S ABOUT IT.

CONGRATULATIONS, YOU'VE REACHED THE END OF THE BOOK.

THAT WASN'T SO BAD...

I LIKED THE FLIP BOOK, ANYWAY.

THE REST OF IT WAS KIND OF... MEH...

NOW YOU KNOW EVERYTHING THERE IS TO KNOW ABOUT CREATIVE TEEN PROGRAMMING IN LIBRARIES.

REALLY? THAT'S ALL THERE IS?

NO, OF COURSE NOT. I WAS BEING SARCASTIC.

WE'VE BARELY SCRATCHED THE SURFACE OF CREATIVE PROGRAMMING.

AW, MAN!

I THOUGHT WE WERE ALL DONE.

WE ARE FAR FROM ALL DONE.

THE POSSIBILITIES FOR CREATIVE PROGRAMMING ARE INFINITE!

INFINITE?!

BUT WE'RE PRACTICALLY AT THE END OF THE BOOK!

THERE'S ONLY A COUPLE OF PAGES LEFT!

FOR THE PURPOSES OF THIS BOOK, WE'RE JUST ABOUT DONE. BUT BEFORE WE LITERALLY CLOSE THE BOOK ON THE SUBJECT, I WANT TO OPEN EVERYONE'S MIND TO ALL THE POSSIBILITIES OUT THERE FOR CREATIVE PROGRAMMING WITH TEENS.

BUT HOW ARE YOU GOING TO COVER AN INFINITE NUMBER OF POSSIBILITIES? IT CAN'T BE DONE.

OH, BUT ON THE CONTRARY, IT CAN BE DONE.

LET ME INTRODUCE YOU TO A LITTLE SOMETHING CALLED...

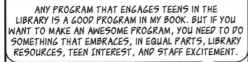

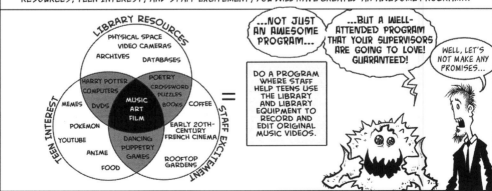

From *Murder Mystery, Graphic Novels, and More: Innovative Programs for Engaging Teens in Your Library* by Thane Benson. Santa Barbara, CA: Libraries Unlimited. Copyright © 2019.

About the Author

THANE BENSON is a librarian for Denver Public Library in Denver, Colorado. He specializes in working with teens to create original programming that fosters creativity and encourages expression. When he is not at the library, Thane moonlights as an independent comic book and graphic novel creator. He is the creator of the graphic novel *Burnt*, the comic book series *Quick: The Clockwork Knight*, the comic strip *Mr. Skizz*, and the ongoing webcomic *HellHole*, which updates weekly at www.thanebenson.com.